Reinventing the Classroom Experience

Learn how to design versatile learning environments in which instruction is as effective virtually as it is in person. Bestselling author and consultant Nancy Sulla shows how you can reinvent the classroom experience and provide high-quality instruction that works as well at home as it does in school. You will discover how to help students build strong work habits and empower them to take responsibility for their learning; five key types of instructional activities; the power of PBL to increase student engagement and motivation; and five types of synchronous engagement between teachers and students. You will also gain strategies for building social and emotional learning, positioning the teacher as the facilitator of learning and parents as partners, and keeping equity at the forefront. No matter what grade level you teach or whether you are teaching fully in school, remotely, or a combination of both, this essential book will help you understand the key structures and strategies that work so students are positioned to learn anywhere, anytime.

Nancy Sulla is an author, national speaker, and thought leader in transforming learning environments to build student engagement, empowerment, and efficacy. She is also the host of the internet TV show "Learning Unwrapped." As the creator of the *Learner-Active, Technology-Infused Classroom*™ and founder of IDE Corp. (Innovative Designs for Education) and EdQuiddity Inc, Dr. Sulla leads her educational consulting firms in the pursuit of equity-focused instructional design, positioning students to change the world. Learn more at nancysulla.com.

Reinventing the Classroom Experience

Learning Anywhere, Anytime

Nancy Sulla

Routledge
Taylor & Francis Group

NEW YORK AND LONDON

First published 2021
by Routledge
605 Third Avenue, New York, NY 10158

and by Routledge
2 Park Square, Milton Park, Abingdon, Oxon, OX14 4RN

Routledge is an imprint of the Taylor & Francis Group, an informa business

Library of Congress Cataloging-in-Publication Data
Names: Sulla, Nancy, author.
Title: Reinventing the classroom experience : learning anywhere, anytime /
    Nancy Sulla.
Description: First Edition. | New York : Routledge, 2021.
Identifiers: LCCN 2021001711 (print) | LCCN 2021001712 (ebook) |
    ISBN 9780367635992 (Hardback) | ISBN 9780367622183 (Paperback) |
    ISBN 9781003119890 (eBook)
Subjects: LCSH: Teachers—Training of. | Blended learning. | Effective
    teaching. | Computer-assisted instruction. | Internet in education. |
    Education—Parent participation.
Classification: LCC LB1707 .S886 2021 (print) | LCC LB1707 (ebook) |
    DDC 370.71/1—dc23
LC record available at https://lccn.loc.gov/2021001711
LC ebook record available at https://lccn.loc.gov/2021001712

ISBN: 978-0-367-63599-2 (hbk)
ISBN: 978-0-367-62218-3 (pbk)
ISBN: 978-1-003-11989-0 (ebk)

Typeset in Palatino
by Apex CoVantage, LLC

Cover image by India L. Adolfsson

To the educators, parents, and students of the 2020 pandemic, for charting an innovative course for the future of education in the face of great challenges. You rock!

To a loving and all-inclusive God who guides my steps daily and who is much greater than any one religion can comprehend.

Contents

Acknowledgments

Thanks to Team Awesome: my smart, innovative, dedicated, and caring colleagues at IDE Corp. and EdQuiddity Inc. I am fortunate to have you to inspire me, challenge my thinking, and partner with me to change the world through education. A special shout-out to Tara Tomczyk, my content editor, for, always lovingly, telling me how to express myself better and how to eliminate dangling participles. I continue to be grateful to work with Lauren Davis, my publisher and a great partner in my quest to change the world through education.

When you're writing about education, you need young people to try out your ideas, watch videos, offer advice, and pop into a video meeting to make you smile. Many thanks to the Kids of IDE for always inspiring me to keep working to make the educational world a better place for them to learn: Aiden, Amelia, Alex, Brianne, Catharine, Charlie, Claire, Colleen, Ellie, Erik, Gabriel, Gabriella, George, India, Jack, Jackson, Kyle, Liam H., Liam M., Liv, Logan, Matt, Nellie, Olivia, Savanna, Sophia, Spencer, Sydney, and William. Thanks to India L. Adolfsson, currently a student at F.I.T., for creating graphics for me over the years, including the cover of this book.

Last, but clearly not least, to those who stand up and take action to make all aware of the need for greater justice and inclusion in our society: Black Lives Matter, LGBTQ+, women's rights. Never stop marching! As IDE's EVP and friend, Tanya Bosco, quoting Margaret Mead, often says: "Never doubt that a small group of thoughtful, committed citizens can change the world; indeed, it's the only thing that ever has."

Introduction

The power of school comes not from the content you teach, but from positioning students to learn.

It Takes a Disruptor

Throughout history, major events have disrupted the norm to produce innovation. Learning began through oral traditions, with the African philosopher Imhotep believed to be the first, dating back to 2600 B.C.; followed by the Indian philosophers Yajnavalkya and Shankaracharya; Chinese philosophers Confucius, Sun Tzu, and Lao Tzu; and Greek philosophers Socrates, Plato, and Aristotle. For thousands of years, the earliest teachers spread their knowledge and wisdom through the spoken word, sometimes written down by the students.

The Chinese invention of the printing press in the first century A.D. allowed the first mechanically produced text and began the transformation to learning through the written word. Eighteen centuries later, the Second Industrial Revolution brought the ability to mass-produce products and influenced schooling to become efficient through a systemized, larger-scale delivery of information to students. While the twentieth century brought great technological advances with computers and the internet, nothing seemed to have the power to release schools from the grasp of the factory model of efficiency of information delivery as being paramount to learning.

The year is 2020. The COVID-19 virus has shut down the factories of school. Learning continued for many through the power of technology, though some still had to rely on printed text, in the absence of devices and internet connectivity. The latter have driven stakeholders in some geographic areas to provide more global and universal access to technology. This disruptor can be known in history as either the cause of a brief departure from the factory model of education or the catalyst to reinvent the classroom experience: it's up to you.

#DoSomethingDifferent

The COVID-19 pandemic challenged students, teachers, and parents to identify new ways to provide "schooling" via remote connections. No one could have imagined that schools would close for months, leaving students to learn at home based on remotely delivered lessons. Many viewed technology as the venue through which teachers would deliver instruction much like they did in school, but that didn't work out as well as some had hoped. It is impossible to simply recreate the experience in a brick-and-mortar classroom through technology. The pandemic was a wake-up call for schools: to be prepared to provide high-quality instructional experiences through structures and strategies that work as well at home as they do in school, such that students can learn anywhere, anytime. Schools can't afford to think that what happened in the spring of 2020 can't happen again.

As of 2020, schools were still fashioned to resemble a factory, with students moving from subject to subject, class to class, while teachers filled them with knowledge through lessons. Perhaps it's time, instead to think of schools more like restaurants: dine in or take out—same great food! The point is, we need to be prepared to be able to provide high-quality instruction whether students are in the physical school building or learning at home. It's time for a new normal for school.

Today's educators are part of a generation that has the opportunity to reinvent the classroom experience, taking advantage of what technology has to offer, educators' expertise, and the benefits of both the physical classroom experience and the home-based learning experience. The key is to begin by thinking about how students learn and then adopt structures and strategies that work as well at home as they do in school.

Students Taking Charge

I developed the *Learner-Active, Technology-Infused Classroom* framework in the 1980s, wrote the first *Students Taking Charge* book in 2011, and released the second editions (K–5, 6–8, and leadership) in 2018. The goal of the framework is to build student engagement, empowerment, and efficacy. Much of my consulting career has been dedicated to helping schools implement this framework.

When schools closed in March 2020, I heard from administrators and teachers that students and teachers in *Learner-Active, Technology-Infused Classrooms* shifted to remote teaching and learning with relative ease. Students were already used to taking responsibility for their own learning; they were used to creating a schedule for how they would use their time and then following it; they were used to being engaged and empowered. I was thrilled to hear that.

I realized, though, that the *Learner-Active, Technology-Infused Classroom* framework was designed for the physical classroom. So, I set out to rethink some of the structures and strategies to ensure that they would work as well at home as they do in school. I refer to this collection of structures and strategies as a **Hybrid Learning Environment**. That's not the same as a hybrid attendance model, with students attending the physical school building on alternate days. It's a learning environment that works regardless of where students are, allowing students to learn from home or in school: learning anywhere, anytime.

About the Book Cover

This book is about a revolution: a group of educators around the world who see this moment in time as an opportunity to depart from a former view of the teaching–learning relationship to forge a new path and reinvent the classroom experience. Graphic arts student India L. Adolfsson designed the cover to depict this process of moving from the tightly scheduled learning world of the physical classroom to learning anywhere, anytime.

In the lower left corner, you'll see the icons of physical classrooms over the years. Moving up and to the right, the student leaves the confines of a physical learning environment to enter the world of learning through computer technology, introduced into schools in the 1980s. The late 1990s ushered in the advent of wireless technology, allowing students to take those computing devices with them. Along with that came the ability to connect with others through social media. Ultimately, the World Wide Web has connected students to information and others around the world. While these technology capabilities have existed for years, perhaps now is the time students will be able to climb out of the physical classroom to venture into the world of learning anywhere, anytime.

How to Read This Book

This book offers you structures, strategies, examples, and insights for several topics critical to a learning environment, whether fully in school, fully at home, or a combination of both:

◆ Chapter 1: Do Something Different — a look at seven attributes of a reinvented classroom experience

- ◆ Chapter 2: Positioning Students for Success—structures for building strong work habits
- ◆ Chapter 3: Positioning Students for Independent Learning—structures for empowering students to take responsibility for their own learning, including five types of instructional activities
- ◆ Chapter 4: Fueling All Learning—the power of the five Ps of PBL (problem-based, project-based, place-based, profession-based, and pursuit-based learning) to increase student engagement and motivation
- ◆ Chapter 5: You're On—five types of synchronous engagement between teachers and students
- ◆ Chapter 6: School Starts With "S" for Social—structures and strategies for building social and emotional learning
- ◆ Chapter 7: Teacher as GPS—the important role of the teacher as facilitator of learning
- ◆ Chapter 8: In Pursuit of Equity—seven lenses of equity through which to view the learning environment
- ◆ Chapter 9: The Home Connection—eight elements of a home-based learning environment to position parents as partners

While the chapters reference one another, there is no specific, intended order. I recommend reading Chapter 1 and then letting your curiosity lead the way through the rest of the book in whatever order you prefer.

All the structures and strategies of a **Hybrid Learning Environment** are represented as capitalized and italicized words. They can become a checklist, of sorts, for your reinvented classroom experience. (For those of you familiar with the *Learner-Active, Technology-Infused Classroom*, you'll recognize most of the structures and strategies—and notice a few new ones.)

Confucius said, "By three methods we may learn wisdom: first, by reflection, which is noblest; second, by imitation, which is easiest; and third, by experience, which is bitterest." Sticking with the noblest route to wisdom, while you are reading, you will be asked to stop and reflect using an *Efficacy Notebook*. Please set that up in advance, guided by the next section.

The *Efficacy Notebook*

One of the structures we use to promote high levels of retained learning in the *Learner-Active, Technology-Infused Classroom* (LATIC) (Sulla, 2019a, 2019b) is the *Efficacy Notebook*. Unlike a typical notebook that is meant as a repository for notes, the *Efficacy Notebook* is a powerful tool to solidify learning and the realization that we learn in order to accomplish much greater challenges. Essentially, when students complete a *Learning Activity* or assignment, they add it to their *Efficacy Notebook* (which can be paper or digital). They then stop before compliantly moving on to the next activity. They summarize what they learned and then answer questions, such as:

- ◆ How will this learning help you in solving the bigger problem-based task on which you are working?
- ◆ How does this learning relate to other concepts and skills you have learned?
- ◆ What else would you like to know about this topic?

For your journey through this book, please obtain either a paper notebook or journal or establish a digital document. Add your name and the name of this book. Start with your first entry by answering these questions:

1 Why did you choose to read this book?
2 What do you hope to learn from it?
3 What are some of your current successes in promoting student learning?
4 What are some of your current challenges in promoting student learning?

The power of school comes not from the content you teach but from positioning students to learn: anywhere, anytime. That's what this book is all about! On to Chapter 1. . . .

References

Sulla, N. (2019a). *Students taking charge in grades K–5: Inside the learner-active, technology-infused classroom*. New York: Routledge.

Sulla, N. (2019b). *Students taking charge in grades 6–12: Inside the learner-active, technology-infused classroom*. New York: Routledge.

1

Do Something Different

You have a unique opportunity to reinvent the teaching–learning relationship for students for the ages.

 Imagine!

Imagine when people hear the word "school," they no longer have a mental image of a building teeming with students, teachers, and administrators. Rather, they see a learning environment characterized by teachers providing online and in-person support whether students are at home or in school; students' brains being challenged and maturing, no matter where they are learning; students building self-esteem and efficacy; teachers and parents working as partners in students' academic, social, physical, and emotional growth; students working on real-world problems of interest beyond the "school day."

*This needs to be our new norm, the reality for "schooling" in the twenty-first century. It's time to reinvent the classroom experience to serve an ever-evolving society. Whether the result of a virus shutdown, reaching geographically distant students, allowing parents to travel with their children during the school year, addressing the needs of homebound students, or any other need, the move for schools to offer students the ability to learn from school or home is a powerful, much-needed shift in the field of education. Now, more than ever, school means that students are learning in varied environments: at home, in school, or a combination of both. Flexible learning environments allow students to engage in "learning anywhere, anytime." Welcome to the **Hybrid Learning Environment** ! That doesn't mean students have to be split between school and home in a hybrid attendance model. It means that the structures* *and strategies in your students' reinvented classroom experience work as well whether students are at home or at school, and students' transition from one venue to the other is seamless. It's about learning anywhere, anytime.*

Creative Roots

Let me take you back in time. The year is 1666. A young man was a student at Trinity College in Cambridge, England. With the outbreak of the Great Plague of London (the last epidemic of the bubonic plague), Cambridge sent students home to socially distance. While home, this young man was outside by an apple tree, perhaps for some fresh air or shade while reading, when an apple fell from the tree. He mused over why it fell to the ground and not sideways or up. That moment set Isaac Newton to working on his theories of gravity. During his social distancing, he went on to develop theories of motion and optics and developed the foundations of calculus. Physics was born! A pandemic can be a disruptor from which creativity flourishes.

In times of stress and uncertainty, the mind becomes more creative, as it seeks to resolve all the unknowns. The pandemic of 2020 gave rise to new ideas for the teaching–learning relationship out of the necessity of social distancing. It's time for us to follow Sir Isaac Newton's lead, look around at the possibilities, and think outside the box. #DoSomethingDifferent.

I remember . . . at age 12 starting a neighborhood summer school three mornings a week. I had students ranging from a gifted 3-year-old to an 18-year-old with cerebral palsy who looked forward to the social interaction. For parents, I was providing babysitting services, but I was serious about schooling. I decided to engage my students in collaborative problem solving. They worked as one community of learners; I held them accountable to my high expectations; my end-of-summer graduation ceremony was filled with efficacious students and grateful parents. Apparently, #DoSomethingDifferent is in my blood. Thank you to all my "first" students. I'm happy to report that 3-year-old Bobby is now a judge in Norway; and I'm dedicated to changing the world through education.

Three Clear Goals for a New Generation

Every teacher should have three clear goals: academic learning, social and emotional learning (SEL), and efficacy — positioning students to tackle any goal, challenge, or problem. How do you get there? Well, *that* is the subject of this book. Refrain from simply replicating what school used to look like, for example, simply live-streaming lessons you used to offer in the classroom. Instead, develop new structures and strategies to achieve these goals.

People born roughly between the years 2001 and 2018 are known as Generation Z; they follow the Baby Boomers, Generation X, and Generation Y (Millennials). They are the children of Generation X and Generation Y. In their book, *Generation Z Unfiltered* (2019), Tim Elmore and Andrew McPeak offer seven characteristics of this generation and implore us to partner with them to help them learn and mature in their early lives. They are:

◆ *More private*—Learning from the mistakes of the millennial generation, they use social media in ways that protect their content.

◆ *More anxious*—Life is easier and yet harder than prior generations; they "suffer from more mental health problems than any other generation of kids" (p. 28).

◆ *More restless*—Their self-images are often shaped through social media and are constantly shifting based on interests and situations.

◆ *More tech savvy*—They spend a significant amount of time online and multitask using multiple devices. As a result, they often prefer to learn alone, using technology.

◆ *More nurtured*—Given the level of information and access to knowledge available to them, their parents are even more focused on protecting them than previous generations. "Parents became helicopters as they raised the Millennial generation. They have become Snowplows now that they're raising Gen Z" (p. 29).

◆ *More entrepreneurial*—Having lived through two recessions since 2000, they are not inclined to focus on getting that good job as much as they are on starting their own business from home.

◆ *More redemptive*—They value inclusivity and acceptance of all people; equality and respect are very important to them. "They believe they can change the world because they've grown up in a world that is already changing" (p. 31).

Consider the convergence of the three goals of academics, SEL, and efficacy with Generation Z and the world of teaching through a post-pandemic. This is the time to design learning for a new generation in a new time in our society. #DoSomethingDifferent.

> **STOP! Turn to Your *Efficacy Notebook* (See the Introduction)**
> The book *Generation Z Unfiltered* (Elmore & McPeak, 2019) was published a year before the COVID-19 pandemic of 2020. Consider each of the previous characteristics, copy them into your *Efficacy Notebook*, and add your thoughts about how the pandemic, and teaching and learning through the pandemic, may be further shaping this generation of students.

Do Something Different

The future of education is not in the brick-and-mortar classroom, nor is it in remote, computer-aided instruction. The future of education is in designing learning environments that allow students to work at home or in school and, if they have access to both, move seamlessly between the two, having the same structures and strategies apply in both venues. The future of education is in learning anywhere, anytime.

Having students follow one set of procedures in the physical classroom and another at home is counterproductive to learning. The student then has to put brainpower into considering how to accomplish a task based on physicality. Consider something as simple as raising one's hand or walking over to the teacher to ask for help. That works in the physical classroom but not at home. In the *Learner-Active, Technology-Infused Classroom*, or LATIC (Sulla, 2011), the teacher establishes a *Help Board* where students, once having exhausted other resources for obtaining help—such as checking for tools or documents in the *Resource Area* and requesting assistance from *Peer Experts*—write their names on the *Help Board*. As the teacher moves from student to student, facilitating instruction, they glance at the *Help Board* to see if anyone needs immediate assistance. When school shifted to a remote environment in the spring of 2020, LATIC teachers created digital *Help Boards* to which students posted their names and help topic. What happens if students are sometimes in school and sometimes at home? If their brains have to keep shifting between "school means I write my name on the board" and "home means I write my name in the digital document," they will lose precious time that could be focused on learning. In a **Hybrid Learning Environment**, the teacher uses a digital *Help Board*, whether students are at home or in school. In school, the teacher might project the *Help Board* to make it easier to see, at any moment, who needs help; that digital *Help Board* would include names of both students who are physically in the classroom and those at home. Hybridity is about striking a balance between best practices in a physical classroom and best practices in a remote classroom such that they work easily in both environments.

Positioning Yourself to Reinvent the Classroom

Educators put a lot of time and energy into the instructional side of school, with the major areas being:

- Whole-group and small-group "synchronous" instruction
- Student assignments and instructional activities
- Formative and summative assessment
- Collaboration and SEL
- Student responsibility and executive function
- Partnering with parents

You address these areas through lesson planning, classroom norms and structures, professional-development offerings, Professional Learning Community (PLC) meetings, and faculty meetings. In a **Hybrid Learning Environment**, you need to meld the best practices related to these topics used in the physical classroom and the best practices used in remote teaching and learning. Then, you need to consider what else you can do and what you can do differently. What could you do that you've never done before to promote academic learning, SEL, and efficacy for *all* your students? Let the disruptor pandemic cause your creativity to flourish as you think about doing something different.

As you tackle reinventing the classroom experience, you'll refer to seven attributes of a **Hybrid Learning Environment** that will ensure all students are engaged in academic, social, physical, and emotional growth through a powerful learning environment.

A Quick Look at the Hybrid Learning Environment Framework

The seven attributes of a **Hybrid Learning Environment** will position students to succeed in anywhere, anytime learning. Teachers are the main curators, students are co-creators, and parents play an important role in helping their children create a productive home-based learning environment. Read through the descriptions and consider the questions posed in Table 1.1.

Table 1.1 Seven Attributes of a Hybrid Learning Environment

An atmosphere of continual motivation	An "atmosphere" is an overall feeling and/or effect of a place. How will you create an overall feeling of motivation in your physical and remote classroom?
A landscape of opportunities for academically rigorous learning	A "landscape" consists of the prevailing conditions in a particular place. How will you ensure that the prevailing conditions of your physical and remote classroom are always geared toward academically rigorous learning?
A climate of executive function	A "climate" represents any conditions that have a widespread effect on life, activity, etc. How will you create the conditions under which students will continuously build executive function in your physical and remote classroom?
A culture of social and emotional learning	A "culture" is evidenced by the ideas, customs, skills, arts, etc., of a people or group that are transferred, communicated, or passed along. How will you position the competencies of social and emotional learning (www. casel.org) to represent the way of life in your physical and remote classroom?
A foundation of student responsibility for learning	A "foundation" is the base upon which something rests. How will you fill your physical and remote classroom with the structures and strategies to create a clear background for students taking responsibility for their own learning?
A network of purposeful and productive facilitation of learning	A "network" can be defined as an extended group of people with similar interests or concerns who interact and remain in contact for mutual assistance or support. How will you develop interactions among people in your physical and remote classroom to facilitate learning?
A structure of meaningful, data-driven learning	A "structure" is the purposeful arrangement of all the parts of a whole. How will you purposefully arrange a collection of structures and strategies for both educators and students to use data to drive learning in both your physical and remote classroom?

Note: The above framework definitions referenced are from yourdictionary.com.

> **STOP! Turn to Your *Efficacy Notebook***
>
> Put this table into your *Efficacy Notebook*. You may take a photo and insert it, type just the headings into a table, or use another way to capture it. Then, answer the following questions.
>
> 1 How do you currently accomplish each of these attributes?
> 2 What ideas come to mind for each while reading?
> 3 What related questions do you want answered in reading this book?
> 4 Why do you think any or each of these is important for Generation Z students?

Intentional Instructional Design

The fact is, as a teacher, you are a caretaker of children's minds. You are not merely an information disseminator; you work to determine the best approach to ensure that each and every student learns. That means you think about how you present information; assess student progress; address students' emotional, social, and physical well-being; and build executive function, which has an impact on student achievement (Sulla, 2018). Some structures and strategies are effective in a brick-and-mortar classroom; some are effective in a remote classroom. Rather than developing two different approaches to teaching and learning, develop one hybrid approach that will offer the best learning experience regardless of the venue. The attributes presented earlier will serve as your guide as you do. Each structure you create, action you take, and word you say should be intentionally selected to promote hybridity while advancing academic learning, SEL, and efficacy.

The Need for Clarity

You can provide high-quality learning activities in either venue; however, in a remote venue, it is important to offer very clear steps and directions since you are not readily available to clarify. With the youngest learners, you will need to rely on video recordings and connections for that. You will need to build in supports for English Language Learners (ELLs) and special education students, again through video recordings and connections. Still, that level of direction would benefit students in the physical classroom as well; so, design learning activities that will work in both venues. Your effort will reap benefits regardless of where students are learning.

The Pieces Are Still Here

You will still use many of the structures and strategies, perhaps modified, that you have used in the past, plus new ones. You will still provide instruction, but you will expand your view of what that looks like. You will still assess student progress and use data to inform your instructional decisions, but it will look slightly different to account for the location of the student and teacher at the time. You're not losing a past; you're gaining a future!

You will still connect with small groups of students who share a particular need to be offered direct instruction either through a *Small-Group Mini-Lesson* in a physical venue or the same through a videoconferencing platform in a remote venue. With only five students around a table, on camera, or as a combination of both, the chances are good that you will offer a meaningful lesson that produces learning in either venue. You will still assign purposeful homework in both venues, keeping in mind that it is important to offer students time between learning during the school day and practicing in the evening: a key purpose of homework.

I hope you see that with some modifications to both the brick-and-mortar approach to teaching and remote teaching, you actually have the opportunity to develop one awesome **Hybrid Learning Model**!

A Closer Look at the Seven Attributes

Motivation

At the root of all learning is motivation, whether intrinsic or extrinsic. Intrinsic motivation that is derived from interests, for example, is preferred over extrinsic motivation that is derived from peer pressure, external rewards, and fear. That's because intrinsic motivation will keep fueling the learner and position them well for life, whereas extrinsic motivation relies on others to maintain that motivation. In schools, it's easy to take for granted that students should just be motivated "because." But that's not true of anyone's motivation, whether a student sitting in a classroom, an adult in a staff development day session, or you reading this book! Hey, are you still here???;)

In a brick-and-mortar classroom, you can nudge some students by praising the work they are doing in the moment. Their motivation will either be intrinsically bound to how good it feels to achieve or extrinsically bound to pleasing you as the teacher. That latter strategy, however, is more difficult in a remote venue in which you are not always watching them work.

Teachers can't make students learn. Human beings consciously *choose* to learn, and usually because they have a "felt need" (Sulla, 2019a, 2019b) for the information. Thus, motivation is key to learning. Teachers tap into intrinsic motivation when they allow students to identify real-world problems they want to solve, pursue learning around an interest of theirs, self-assess and set goals, and teach and help others. Teachers also tap into intrinsic motivation when they pose questions that intrigue students and leave them wanting more. Through both the ways in which teachers frame the learning (e.g., through problems and challenges) and the ways in which they facilitate student learning, students can experience an overall feeling of continuous motivation, whether in a physical or remote classroom.

Think of the strategies you currently employ to build student motivation. For your **Hybrid Learning Environment**, think about how you can foster an **atmosphere of continual motivation**, whether in physical or remote venues. You'll dive into this more throughout Chapters 3, 4, and 7.

Opportunities for Academically Rigorous Learning

Academic rigor speaks to a high level of intellectual and academic challenge; it is what makes content meaningful beyond school and valuable in life. The structures of schooling in the past have relied on compliance: students simply doing what they are told. Teaching through compliance works better in the physical classroom than at home, where students are out of the teacher's easy view. Still, teaching through compliance may produce completed assignments but does not necessarily produce long-term learning. Student engagement is the first step to producing long-term learning, whether in a physical classroom or through a remote environment: not "hands-on" entertainment, but brain-challenging, "minds-on" activities that students *want* to tackle.

Different students need different activities as they engage in purposeful learning. Students most likely are at different cognitive levels of readiness; have different cultural backgrounds; may have language barriers; may have learning disabilities that require specialized activities; and definitely have preferred learning styles (i.e., auditory, kinesthetic, and visual, at the simplest level). While it can be hard to provide a variety of different learning activities when attempting to teach an entire class of students, when you shift your thinking to "learning anywhere, anytime," you create that collection of opportunities for students to learn. Students can access more choices that best suit their needs, whether they are in school or at home. With technology available, students can access myriad instructional resources. Learning is most purposeful when the teacher uses all that is available to *curate* a set of *Learning Activities* and helps students select the right activities for their personalized goals.

The key is to ensure students are not frustrated. This requires providing students with differentiated learning activities that allow them to level up

(Prensky, 2006) a step at a time to achieve increasingly higher levels of rigor. That **landscape of opportunities for academically rigorous learning** adds to the **atmosphere of continual motivation** because students are empowered to access various *Learning Activities* that suit their needs. You'll explore these ideas more in Chapters 3 and 7.

Executive Function

What does it take for students to succeed in learning in a physical classroom? How about focusing, shifting attention from one activity to another, working toward a goal, persisting in a task, catching and correcting errors, managing time? These are important skills for being able to work in a physical classroom and are even more important when working from home, where the teacher is not always watching and prompting students to stay on task and make good decisions. These are just a sampling of the skills of executive function, which has a widespread effect on academic achievement, as well as on social and emotional learning. If climate describes the conditions that have a widespread effect on life, activity, etc., then executive function *is* the climate of a learning environment! If you prioritize executive function early in the school year and throughout, you will provide students with a better chance of succeeding in school and life.

Creating a **climate of executive function** helps develop the brain and contributes to stronger academic achievement, which is critical if students are to be self-directed, productive, resourceful, and resilient at home as well as in the physical classroom. Executive function will help students take advantage of a **landscape of opportunities for academically rigorous learning** and feel successful, which will contribute to an **atmosphere of continual motivation**. You'll explore more about executive function in Chapter 6.

Social and Emotional Learning

The five competencies of SEL, as defined by the Collaborative for Academic, Social, and Emotional Learning (www.casel.org), are: self-awareness, self-management, social awareness, relationship skills, and responsible decision-making. All of these depend upon executive function being applied to intrapersonal and interpersonal relationships. Whether students are working independently or collaboratively, engaging in reflection or communication, faced with expectations or challenges, and working from home or school, they need to be guided by a "culture" of norms, structures, and protocols that support social and emotional learning.

In a **Hybrid Learning Environment**, students will be connecting with others both in person and via technology. They will, at times, be following a teacher's direct instruction, and at other times, left to navigate learning on their own. The stronger a student's social and emotional learning, the greater their resiliency and resourcefulness, important qualities for learning at home as well as in school. A variety of structures and strategies for self-assessment, group discussions, collaborative work, resilience, and resourcefulness will draw on the **climate of executive function** and contribute to creating that **culture of social and emotional learning**. There's more to come in Chapter 6!

Student Responsibility for Learning

While it can seem easier to simply direct students—when to sit, when to move, when to talk, and so on—a crucial part of a student's path to lifelong efficacy is taking responsibility for their own learning. In a **Hybrid Learning Environment**, where, at times, students are working at home under their own direction, student responsibility becomes the foundation for success. While in the physical classroom, students may benefit from the immediate accessibility of the teacher to clarify and redirect, they need to build the life skill of taking responsibility, whether the teacher is immediately accessible or not. Consider anything you find yourself overtly directing and create a structure to allow students to accomplish it on their own. That includes more clear, printed directions or a *Directions Video*, a *How-To Sheet* or *Instructional Video*, an *Insights Video*, a checklist, etc.

Consider for a moment a teacher in a physical classroom calling out names for students to come to an area of the room to receive instruction. Students learn to simply wait to be told where to go and what to do. Alternatively, if the teacher sets guidelines for students to know when to come to that area of the room, perhaps based on need or student choice, and then students have the responsibility of showing up at the appointed time, students will build much greater responsibility for their own learning and strengthen their executive function.

When students take greater responsibility for their own learning, teachers are freed up to focus on instruction and student learning over classroom management. In a **Hybrid Learning Environment**, where some students may be physically in the classroom while others are at home, empowering students to take responsibility for their own learning becomes even more important. With a strong **foundation of student responsibility for learning**, teachers can engage more in fostering a **landscape of opportunities for academically rigorous learning** through instruction, facilitation, and data collection. You'll explore this attribute in more depth in Chapter 2.

Purposeful and Productive Facilitation of Learning

Teaching is not learning; teaching is an avenue through which one expects that students will learn. While direct instruction from a teacher, in person or through video, is a part of that process, and independent instructional activities and assignments are a part of that process, the part that has the biggest impact is the purposeful and productive facilitation of learning by a masterful teacher. That's where there can be an assurance that students are engaged in the best instructional activities and assignments to meet their needs.

As students engage in various instructional activities, the teacher's focus turns to the work being produced and the learner in the midst of the process. "Purposeful" means that teachers' focus, questions, and comments fit into a bigger picture. That might be related to content itself: has the student mastered the prerequisite skills to tackle this skill or concept? It might be related to the learning process: has the student selected the best learning activities, place in which to work, and/or peers with whom to work? "Productive" means that the teacher's facilitation has a positive effect on the student's progress.

In a **Hybrid Learning Environment**, teachers create a **network of purposeful and productive facilitation of learning** that includes teachers, co-teachers, teaching assistants, students themselves, administrators, peers, and parents/caregivers. Everyone can and should play a role in facilitating rigorous learning. Develop strategies and structures to advance student learning through two key questions: is the student succeeding with the current instructional activities and assignments? Is the student making the best choices as to how, when, where, and with whom to learn? Your answers will allow you to intervene and guide students in both content and process so they can take appropriate advantage of the **landscape of opportunities for academically rigorous learning** and build a stronger **climate of executive function** and **foundation of student responsibility for learning**. You'll delve more deeply into creating a **network of purposeful and productive facilitation of learning** in Chapter 7.

Meaningful, Data-Driven Learning

Teachers use data to make decisions about instructional lessons and activities. In a **Hybrid Learning Environment**, where students may be in school or at home, data become even more important to maintain an **atmosphere of continual motivation**.

Data can be gathered in a variety of ways, from one-on-one interactions with a student, observation, student work, quizzes, student self-reporting, parent/caregiver input, and more. In a **Hybrid Learning Environment**, data are even more important, as the teacher is sometimes guiding a student who is not physically nearby to observe. Deliberate and purposeful data collection and use contributes to a **structure of meaningful, data-driven learning**.

Teachers use data to inform instruction: modifying plans for individual students; recording additional lessons; designing additional instructional activities; planning for *Small-Group Mini-Lessons*; and more. In a **Hybrid Learning Environment**, data collection and use contribute to a stronger **network of purposeful and productive facilitation of learning**. Positioning students to collect data and reflect contributes to the **culture of social and emotional learning**. You'll explore more on the power of data in Chapters 3 and 7.

Embedded Topics

Many important topics in curriculum and instruction will cross all seven attributes of a **Hybrid Learning Environment**. Following are just a few.

A Time to Effectively Address Equity

Treating all students equally means providing them with the same opportunities, lessons, assessments, and so forth. There is some sense of "fairness" in that. However, equality will not ensure that all students will learn at high levels. Students have different needs beyond the typical differentiation goals of cognitive leveling and learning styles. What matters is equity—providing students with what *they* each need to excel—and, more importantly, justice—revamping the systems that perpetuate issues of inequity.

It is well known that the current model of education, with the teacher center stage, students compartmentalized into age-based groups learning one subject after another in succession across a day, and an emphasis on equal access to education, is based on a factory model of efficiency of years passed. In a factory, sameness is valued; quality control focuses on that sameness. Our current educational model based on factory efficiency has been, for decades, perhaps centuries, an immovable object. While slight changes and adjustments are made, the overall *thinking* behind this efficiency-and-sameness model has not.

The racial and cultural makeup of the world, however, is changing. Modern technology and transportation have allowed people to travel the world and relocate to any land, allowing for a global migration. The "sameness" that once characterized geographic areas has given way to tremendous diversity. And that diversity is pushing at the "sameness" approach to schooling. Some cultures are more individualistic; some are more collaborative; some are more text-dependent; some are more steeped in oral traditions; all have unique attributes that shape people's worldview. It is time for schools not just to "embrace" diversity, as diversity is not an object or ideal. It is time for schools to "reflect" the diversity of their student population in all aspects of school structures, strategies, resources, and policies.

The disruptive nature of the 2020 pandemic provided schools with a compelling reason to change. And one of those changes needed to be the reflection of global diversity in our learning environments. Equity will be addressed in every chapter, with a particular emphasis in Chapter 8.

Co-Teaching

When co-teachers share responsibility for designing and implementing the learning environment, students benefit from the added expertise and attention. In a **Hybrid Learning Environment**, teachers can more easily address the needs of students, whether they are at home or at school. One teacher can be providing small-group instruction while the other connects with students individually, whether at home or at school. One teacher can be videoconferencing with students while the other is reviewing students' online work and offering comments in the midst of students completing assignments. Co-teachers can share responsibility for designing and recording content lessons. Co-teachers do need to share plans and data regularly to ensure that they deliver instruction and facilitate learning in ways that demonstrate seamless collaboration; technology provides myriad opportunities for that.

Collegiality

Teachers usually work together in PLCs or grade/subject-specific teams. This needs to continue with **Hybridity**, considering ways in which teams work that will allow teachers to move seamlessly between school and home. That means most of the materials, agendas, notes, and the like should be stored online, easily accessible wherever the teachers are. It also means the groups should set norms for participation and engagement that can be implemented as easily at home or at school.

Additionally, discussions among colleagues should include the successes and challenges of designing **Hybrid Learning Environments**. Now, more than ever, teachers need to share their ideas, materials, and experiences with their colleagues. Reinventing the classroom will not happen overnight; yet it needs to happen quickly for the good of the students. Develop ways to leverage collegiality for enhanced learning. Teachers can take responsibility for recording lessons that can be used across the grade level or department; they can share graphic organizers and other structures that they find to be successful.

An added attraction of a **Hybrid Learning Environment** is that it is easy to work across "classrooms," with teachers and students using video connections to work together. Students are typically motivated to work with students in other grade levels or schools. The use of technology makes that much easier to accomplish. Teachers and students can benefit from the expanded access to others around the world.

Grading

Grading needs to be redefined in a **Hybrid Learning Environment**. The idea that a grade is what a student *earns* and not what a teacher *gives* becomes more important in a **Hybrid Learning Environment**. Yet, still, the student is only able to earn that grade because a teacher is curating the most effective learning environment for each student. The paradox is that students' grades really reflect the teacher's ability to teach! That may sound harsh, but you'll read in Chapter 6 that the part of the brain that handles higher-level reasoning, responsibility, and accountability does not fully mature until approximately age 25. So, while students certainly need to be held accountable for their actions, schools cannot assume that it is enough to provide students with opportunity and access, and if they fail, it's on them. For grades to be meaningful, schools need to take into account that they represent the level of success of two people in the equation: the student and the teacher.

Grading should begin with clear expectations that are shared with the student. In the early stages of learning new content, students should be involved in self-assessment and goal-setting. The focus should be on students demonstrating that they have achieved content mastery. This may include performance-based assessments where students must apply learning to a new situation.

Grades cannot afford to be modified based on students' home situations; teachers need to provide a learning environment that works in any situation. The goal is to ensure that students learn. When that goal is achieved, grades are high, and deservedly so. If a teacher is successful in designing an effective **Hybrid Learning Environment**, students should all be achieving at a high level.

Parent/Caregiver Communication

Parents and caregivers become partners in a **Hybrid Learning Environment**; after all, they establish the home-based learning environment that plays a role in students' learning. Communication should be ongoing, two-way, and enhanced by technology.

The more parents and caregivers know about the learning activities, assignments, and upcoming deadlines, the better. The more teachers communicate with parents about their role (i.e., they are not the teacher, they are the manager of the home-based learning environment), the easier it will be for parents and caregivers to participate in meaningful ways in their children's learning paths. The more teachers know about parents' and caregivers' situations (e.g., working at home or away from home, number of children in the house, number of computing devices available) the better able they will be to meet the needs of their students.

Hybridity in Action

Armed with the seven attributes of a **Hybrid Learning Environment**, you can now reflect on your current "classroom" and, through reading this book, apply the structures and strategies that you feel will enhance it. A great start is to visualize: close your eyes, and walk yourself mentally through your day. What happens first? Then what? What actions do you take? What words do you speak? What do your students do? As you think through each moment, ask yourself if you have all the structures and strategies set to work as well at home as they do in school. To what extent does your "classroom" address the seven attributes of a **Hybrid Learning Environment**? It may take many iterations to get your "classroom" to where you want it to be, but remember, you are reinventing "school" for today and the future. You have a unique opportunity to reinvent the teaching–learning relationship for students for the ages. Your **Hybrid Learning Environment** will pave the way for generations of teachers who follow you.

STOP! Turn to Your _Efficacy Notebook_

Think of a typical day of school (not the first day, though you can use that for a second round of this activity). Write about what happens directly before the start of the day or class period, during that time, and after that time. Describe in as much detail as possible what a half-hour or hour is like. Then, answer the following questions.

1   What are some examples of structures and strategies you use that work in a **Hybrid Learning Environment** as well at home as they do in school?
2   Which of the seven attributes of a **Hybrid Learning Environment** resonate most with you? Which will be most challenging?
3   What are some ideas you have for structures and strategies that you want to include in your **Hybrid Learning Environment**?
4   What questions do you have that you hope are answered in the rest of the book?

References

Elmore, T., & McPeak, A. (2019). *Generation z unfiltered*. Atlanta, GA: Poet Gardener.

Prensky, M. (2006). *Don't bother me, mom, I'm learning*. St. Paul, MN: Paragon.

Sulla, N. (2011). *Students taking charge: Inside the learner-active, technology-infused classroom*. New York: Routledge.

Sulla, N. (2018). *Building executive function: The missing link to student achievement*. New York: Routledge.

Sulla, N. (2019a). *Students taking charge in grades K–5: Inside the learner-active, technology-infused classroom*. New York: Routledge.

Sulla, N. (2019b). *Students taking charge in grades 6–12: Inside the learner-active, technology-infused classroom*. New York: Routledge.

2

Positioning Students for Success

The power of school comes not from the content you teach, but from positioning students to learn.

 ## Imagine!

Imagine your students join your class, whether in person or virtually, and know exactly what to do to get started on their work. Imagine they follow directions and re-read directions when they're stuck. Imagine they complete work carefully and hand it in on time. Imagine they succeed in grappling with content and pushing through to achieve mastery. Imagine they engage with you in thought-provoking conversations about the content and how they can use it in real life. Imagine they are always prepared for class and always complete their homework. Sound like a dream? It's really more attainable than you may think! You just need to "curate" a collection of structures that will make your students' reinvented classroom experience one that positions them for success! With learning, SEL, and efficacy as your goals, the structures you introduce early on will position students for success.

Put Students in Charge!

With students learning anywhere, anytime, teachers must ensure that students are positioned to learn at high levels no matter where they are, no matter what time they are engaging. Foundational to building a **Hybrid Learning Environment** is positioning students to take charge of their own learning. That begins with the structures introduced in this chapter, but the theme continues throughout the book. Positioning students for success includes doing so in learning and in building the skills of social and emotional learning. Ensuring all students meet with success by positioning them to do so, whatever their backgrounds, whatever their cultures, whatever their current knowledge levels, whatever their learning style preferences, whatever whatever . . . that's equity . . . and equity begins with positioning all students for success! Providing that equitable learning environment to ensure student success supports student efficacy, allowing students to tackle any challenge or pursue any goal with confidence. The power of school comes not from the content you teach, but from positioning students to learn.

I remember . . . when I was in college in the 1970s, studying to become a teacher. I was assigned to spend time observing in a kindergarten open classroom. I was amazed at how the students were so self-directed, empowered! Upon deeper observation, I noticed that each student had a folder created by the teacher with various assignments and worksheets in it. They happily worked on their instructional activities. After school, I asked the teacher how she did it. She admitted that it took her hours every night to create all those folders for her students. I remember at that time thinking that teachers could never sustain that. We needed another way. It was then I became dedicated to putting students in charge of their own learning, so teachers could offer a variety of ways through which to learn but empower the students to make choices and set up their schedules, even the youngest. Thank you to the professors at Fairleigh Dickinson University and the teachers I had the honor of shadowing for inspiring me to think differently from the start of my career!

The *Great Hybrid Learner Rubric*

Many teachers use classroom rules, such as:

- ◆ Come to class prepared;
- ◆ Finish your work on time;
- ◆ Don't call out;
- ◆ Join meetings on time; and
- ◆ Cameras on.

The problem with rules is that they are "binary" —just two options: you either succeed or fail; you follow the rule or break it. As a student, if I remember to bring everything else I need in order to learn but I forget a pencil, I break the rule. If I get excited about something and call out of turn, I break the rule. Consider a different approach that positions students for success at all times. As a teacher, you want to position your students for success in, for example, attending a *Small-Group Mini-Lesson*, whether in class or joining in remotely from home. Suppose you had given students the *Analytic Rubric* row depicted in Table 2.1 at the start of the year. (Early childhood teachers: you'll want to use images, as in the example in Table 2.2.) Note: an *Analytic Rubric*, as opposed to a holistic rubric, is one in which a student can self-evaluate row by row, landing in different columns for each row. The *Practitioner* (or *Practicing*) column is the goal, with some students achieving at the expert column.

Using an *Analytic Rubric* such as the *Great Hybrid Learner Rubric*, students seek to find themselves, celebrate that, and work to move to the next column

Table 2.1 A Row on a *Great Hybrid Learner Rubric*

	Novice	Apprentice	Practitioner	Expert
Attending a Small-Group Mini-Lesson	— with a reminder, joins on time — with a reminder, has notebook and pencil/pen — with prompting, focuses on topic	— usually joins on time or 1–2 minutes early — has notebook and pencil/pen — if remote, with prompting, turns on camera — remains focused on topic during instruction — if remote, with prompting, keeps microphone muted except when speaking	— joins on time or 1–2 minutes early — has notebook, pencil/pen, and any related materials — if remote, turns on camera — remains focused on the topic throughout — engages with questions and answers — if remote, keeps microphone muted except when speaking	all of *Practitioner*, plus takes notes that clearly represent the content presented for future reference

Table 2.2 A Row on a Primary-Level *Great Hybrid Learner Rubric*

	Practicing	Got It!
I am ready to learn.	❏ I have the things I need to learn. pencil book device paper ❏ I have a place to learn. desk table	All of Practicing plus: I help my friends get ready to learn!

on the right. The columns progress from left to right to mirror the direction of reading, and progress. Notice that there is no negative language, no language of failure. Each column to the right presents a next step to achieve beyond what was last accomplished. If I'm usually on time, surely I can figure out how to always be on time! This becomes the daily goal for the student when attending *Small-Group Mini-Lessons*. Using the *Great Hybrid Learner Rubric*, rather than a checklist, positions students for success by allowing them to self-assess, set goals, and work to achieve them in increments toward the ultimate goal. It offers them a more detailed description of what success "looks like."

When you first introduce a *Great Hybrid Learner Rubric*, at the end of a small-group lesson, have students look at it and reflect on how they did that day. At first, you'll need to walk them through the categories. Soon, you'll be able to ask them to refer to their copy of the *Great Hybrid Learner Rubric* and reflect on it. Eventually, this will just be a row on a larger *Great Hybrid Learner Rubric* on which they reflect and self-assess throughout the year. Getting started, you'll need to be deliberate in pointing out the left-to-right progression and help students learn to use it.

For example, for students who struggle with joining in on time, remind them when the meeting is about to start. That will put them in the *Novice* column. Eventually, you can say, "So do you think you need reminders anymore, or can you find a way to remind yourself of our next meeting?" That question allows the student to move to the *Apprentice* column. Facilitate their being able to determine what they need to do to move to the right by commending them on progress and asking specific questions to help them set goals to move more toward the right.

The examples in Tables 2.1 and 2.2 each include just one row; your *Great Hybrid Learner Rubric* will have many rows. See the Appendix for examples of *Great Hybrid Learner Rubrics* across the grade levels.

The Rows

At the youngest levels, you might label your row categories:

- ◆ I Am Ready
- ◆ I Am Responsible for My Work
- ◆ I Can Focus

At elementary levels, you might label your row categories:

- ◆ Establishing Structures
- ◆ Reflection and Self-Assessment
- ◆ Self-Regulation and Focus
- ◆ Working Through Challenges

At secondary levels, you might expand, as students demonstrate basic self-management and engagement skills, to include row categories such as:

- ◆ Resourcefulness
- ◆ Resilience
- ◆ Social Awareness
- ◆ Self-Care
- ◆ Reflection

Design the rows to fit the needs of your students and your program.

The Columns

Note, again, that you don't want to include anything of a negative nature. Each cell (intersection of the row and column) should be criteria to which a student can aspire. As they celebrate, they move to the next column. Consider using the camera in videoconferencing. You would not write "does not turn on camera," as you do not want students to aspire to that. Instead, write positive criteria to which the student can aspire, such as "with prompting, turns on camera." Then build a developmental progression from left to right. For example, at the expert level, you may write "turns off camera if a distraction occurs." As another example, at first, a student focuses on the lesson when prompted by the teacher, which may require multiple reminders throughout the session. The next step would be to remain focused during the instructional portion. Perhaps as other students start asking questions, a student's mind might wander. The next step would be to remain focused throughout. At the highest level, the students' comments and questions are related to those of the teacher and other contributors.

The more you think through the behaviors and work habits you want your students to demonstrate, thus offering them clearly articulated expectations, the more likely they are to meet your expectations. The more you break down these behaviors and habits into small, achievable steps, the more likely students are to be able to achieve, one step at a time. For non-native speakers and students who read below grade level, include images as cues.

Be sure the *Expert* column is a higher-level implementation of the skill, rather than something extraneous. For example, designing a poster of tips for success targets abilities other than the rubric row. While this may be a valuable activity, it does not belong on a rubric where students are self-assessing their abilities based on the row title. You could, however, use *Expert* criteria such as "and explains to others how to . . ." Any time a student can not only demonstrate a skill but break it down and explain it to others, they are demonstrating an advanced understanding. This could involve a product *they* create to demonstrate this ability. Still, if you can, look for a higher level of developmental performance. For example, if my goal is for students to set goals related to work habits, at a beginning level, I may indicate that they set goals related to focus, time management, materials management, and the like; at the expert level, I may indicate that they set goals related to resilience, tenacity, and consensus-building. The key is to keep moving students toward a more complex, higher-order implementation of the skill.

Getting Students Started

Except perhaps at high school and college levels, it may not be useful to simply provide the students with the entire *Great Hybrid Learner Rubric*, as it may be too overwhelming and make it difficult to focus on where to start. For younger students, special education students, and those who lag in the development of executive function, just introduce one row at a time. Explain the criteria, offer examples, and have students discuss what achieving at the *Practitioner* level would look like. Let them set goals for just that one row. Have them assess their progress throughout the day. Make that row the focus of the day or week before introducing the next. Once you do, the student must now attend to two rows, not forgetting about the previous row but adding a second set of criteria. Then introduce the third row, and so forth.

If you are a secondary teacher sharing the full *Great Hybrid Learner Rubric* with your students, allow your special education students to focus on a row at a time. If you think it would be useful, enlarge the font in the rows to make it easier to focus on the words; offer more descriptive words, perhaps with images. The intent is to introduce the *Great Hybrid Learner Rubric* as a positive structure in positioning students for success.

At first, pause often to have students each self-assess and develop just one goal to achieve. Eventually, ask students at the end of each week to reflect on and write about their progress in achieving at the *Practitioner* column of the *Great Hybrid Learner Rubric*. This may become a daily or weekly reflection in the students' digital *Efficacy Notebook*.

As the year progresses, retire certain rows and add rows to allow students to achieve at even more sophisticated aspects of work habits and behavior. While the year may begin with being prepared, focusing on work, and engaging well with others, it may end with collaboration, resilience, and resourcefulness.

The *Great Hybrid Learner Rubric* contributes to the **atmosphere of continual motivation** by offering students a "next step" as they achieve a level of success. It supports a **climate of executive function** and a **culture of social and emotional learning** when you include rows that address related skills. It helps create the **foundation of student responsibility for learning** by positioning them to take greater responsibility for their own learning. It contributes to a **structure of meaningful, data-driven learning** by providing students with a tool for self-assessment from which to set goals. I'm sure you can connect it to the other attributes as well!

The *Great Hybrid Learner Rubric* is a useful structure for building student responsibility and achievement, but there will still be times when students need further assistance in your **Hybrid Learning Environment**. Visualize the student experience throughout the day and create structures to support their success.

STOP! Turn to Your *Efficacy Notebook*

Reflect on this beginning structure—the *Great Hybrid Learner Rubric*—and answer the following questions in your digital or paper *Efficacy Notebook*.

1 How might the *Great Hybrid Learner Rubric* help your students meet with greater success working in your **Hybrid Learning Environment**?
2 What categories might you want to include in your *Great Hybrid Learner Rubric*?
3 How might you use your *Great Hybrid Learner Rubric* with students, parents/caregivers, co-teachers, administrators, and anyone else? What other ideas do you have?

While the *Great Hybrid Learner Rubric* offers students a comprehensive look at successful work habits, there are many other opportunities to create structures to position students for success. Following are just some of the many structures you could use with your students.

Help!

How will students access help when they need it? Design a process for accessing help; include more than just the teacher. For example:

1 Re-read the directions
2 Check our *Resource Area*
3 Look to find a *Peer Expert*
4 Add your name to the *Help Board*

When faced with a question or confusion, the student should always re-read the directions of the current activity first. This could be included in the criteria of the *Great Hybrid Learner Rubric*. If they still have a question or are confused, a digital *Resource Area* might help.

Imagine that you have an instructional activity in which students read a section of text and fill in a graphic organizer. After reading the text passage, some students will figure out the graphic organizer and get started. Others may be a little unsure and want to complete it correctly, so they'd be seeking assurance. Others may have no idea how to fill out the graphic organizer. While in the physical classroom, you can walk over to a student and help;

you don't have that ease in assisting remote students. Still, it is important to build a **foundation of student responsibility for learning** no matter where students are learning. So, instead, to assist any student on this task, create a *Directions Video* to demonstrate how you expect them to fill out the graphic organizer. You might also include a text-based *How-To Sheet*. Both of these could be stored in the digital *Resource Area*. Students who have a question or are confused can first re-read the activity directions and then look in the digital *Resource Area*. What if a student still needs help?

A digital *Peer Expert Board* can prove useful if you first vet students to ensure that they not only understand the content but can teach it to someone else. Vetting a student can be as simple as requiring students to achieve 100% on a quiz and then connecting with them to have them explain the content to you. You can also offer them a set of scenarios to which to respond to see how they would answer various requests for assistance. Whatever means you use, be sure to only select a *Peer Expert* for a skill or concept whom you know will help others well. You then add the student's name to the digital *Peer Expert Board*. The twofold benefit is that students learn well from one another, and teaching others helps solidify learning. However, you don't want *Peer Experts* spending a lot of time helping others rather than completing their own work. Therefore, after a student has spent a day to a week as a *Peer Expert*, have someone else take over that skill or concept.

Being selected as a *Peer Expert* builds confidence; so, work to ensure that all students are named as *Peer Experts* in something over the course of a week or two. (That may mean specifically teaching students a skill in advance to position them for success as *Peer Experts*.) For students who have difficulty in instructional situations, what a win for them to be selected to be a *Peer Expert*. Everyone can become a *Peer Expert* in something!

The digital *Peer Expert Board* will work if students are able to access help from one another. Students in the physical classroom will be able to connect with one another, but whether students can access other students digitally when they are working remotely will depend on your school's policies. Students may be able to chat but not videoconference, for instance, or they may be able to videoconference. You might place willing *Peer Experts* in a room of their own where they are working remotely with a link or room number attached to their name on the digital *Peer Expert Board*.

Back to the students who have questions or are confused. . . . After re-reading the directions, checking in the digital *Resource Area*, and attempting to locate a *Peer Expert*, students who are still stuck should add their names to the digital *Help Board*. A digital *Help Board* is simply a document, perhaps with a table, where students can enter their names and topics for which they need help. (Early childhood teachers: use a document or app where students can drag their picture and name to a specified area on the screen for help.) Students then move on to something else while waiting for help. As the teacher, you check the *Help Board* between working with students or offering small-group lessons to see if anyone needs help. If so, attend to those students. If a student finds help in the meantime, they should delete their request. If another student sees the note and wants to offer help, they can; that is, if you allow that in your classroom.

The *Resource Area*, digital *Help Board*, and the use of *Peer Experts* all work as well at home as they do in school; they play an important role in establishing a **network of purposeful and productive facilitation of learning**. The *Resource Area*, *Peer Experts*, and *Help Board* all encourage students to self-advocate so that they, their peers, and their teachers can help facilitate their learning. Self-advocacy is an important component of a **foundation of student responsibility for learning**.

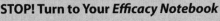

STOP! Turn to Your *Efficacy Notebook*

Reflect on this section on positioning students to advocate for themselves to receive help. Then, answer the following questions in your digital or paper *Efficacy Notebook*.

1   How do your students currently access help when they are stuck?
2   What ideas do you have from this section that you will incorporate into your classroom?
3   Reflect on the seven attributes of a **Hybrid Learning Environment** (listed in Chapter 1). How do the *Resource Area*, *Peer Experts*, and *Help Board* support any or all of the seven attributes?

Protocols

The *Great Hybrid Learner Rubric* offers a student individual norms, or expectations, for work habits and for contributing as a member of a larger learning community. The digital *Help Board* and *Peer Experts* provide assistance in the moment. Now, visualize students engaging with one another to accomplish a task or participate in a discussion. Positioning students to work well as a group should include developing specific protocols, or "norms of engagement."

Develop protocols for when students are working with one another. Essentially, protocols teach students *how* to engage in a discussion, collaborate on a project, peer edit or offer feedback on one another's work, or engage in any situation where more than one person is involved.

Student-led discussions are a powerful part of learning; they can be made even more effective through protocols. For younger readers, the protocol may be as simple as:

1   Wait until both partners have their books and are ready to share.
2   Decide which of you will start.
3   Speaker 1: Share the title of the book you are reading and why you chose it.
4   Speaker 2: Make a comment and ask one question about the book.
5   Speaker 1: Answer the question.
6   Speaker 2: Share the title of the book you are reading and why you chose it.
7   Speaker 1: Make a comment and ask one question about the book.
8   Speaker 2: Answer the question.

Outline the discussion protocol and then teach it to students through a video or a small-group meeting where you model this particular protocol. As students become mature in their reading skills, you create new, more sophisticated protocols. At the upper elementary levels, you might include:

1   Ensure that everyone has a book and their double-entry journal and is ready to start the conversation.
2   Decide who will start by asking a higher-order question related to the reading.
3   Respond to the question being posed and/or to a comment being made, but keep the conversation focused.
4   Watch your air time! Leave time for others to speak.
5   Ensure that everyone speaks. If someone has not had a chance to speak, ask them to share their thoughts.
6   When you only have 5 minutes left, finish by having each group member offer one "takeaway" from the discussion.

As students' reading ability matures at the secondary level, offer them protocols for engaging with one another, as with the previous list, but add to the level of sophistication. For example, include asking one another questions about the connections among the author's tone, theme, setting, and characters, as appropriate to the conversation. Ask them to challenge one another's thinking with their questions and document those questions for later review by you.

If one or more students are engaging through videoconference, build in protocols for that aspect as well. Develop protocols for whole-group, small-group, and pairs engagement via videoconference. Include points such as:

◆ Ensure all cameras are on. If you're in class, you're visible.
◆ Mute your microphone to reduce background noise.
◆ If you have something to add to the conversation, unmute your microphone.
◆ Keep an eye on the microphones so that when someone does unmute, you allow them to speak first.
◆ Once you are finished offering your comment, mute your microphone again.
◆ When speaking, look into the camera so others feel you are looking at them instead of at the screen.

Discussion Symbols

Some videoconference platforms have built-in reaction emoticons to indicate that you approve or have a question. You can, however, create your own to either distribute to students or have them print at home and cut out (see Figure 2.1). In the midst of a discussion, they can hold up an image to represent that they, for example:

◆ Have an idea
◆ Made a connection
◆ Have a question
◆ Disagree
◆ Agree
◆ Like it
◆ Celebrate it
◆ Love it
◆ Need it to be repeated

Printed discussion symbols allow students to communicate in nonverbal ways, which is an important aspect of a discussion in an online environment where delays could have students talking over one another. This is a great way to have students signal that they would like to speak or they desire clarification. It also has the bonus benefit of helping English Language Learners associate an image with a concept, such as I agree, I disagree, I have a question, etc.

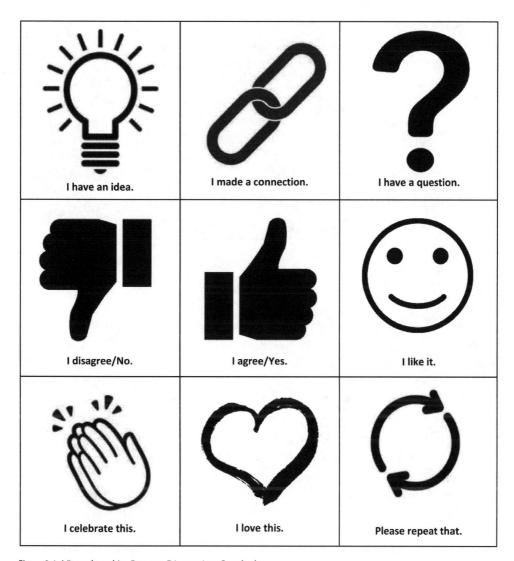

Figure 2.1 Virtual and In-Person Discussion Symbols

This structure can be very useful with younger students and all students as they begin to learn the nuances of online discussion. The next step is to have students learn to unmute to signal their desire to speak and watch the microphones to leave room for those who wish to speak to do so. This builds significant social awareness as well (an SEL competency). Protocols pave the way for more productive student engagement and collaboration with one another.

> **STOP! Turn to Your *Efficacy Notebook***
> Reflect on this section on creating protocols to position students for success in collaborative learning. Then, answer the following questions in your digital or paper *Efficacy Notebook*.
>
> 1 In what ways do students engage with you and others in the classroom for which you could create protocols?
> 2 How do protocols contribute to students learning anywhere, anytime?
> 3 Which of the seven attributes of a **Hybrid Learning Environment** are reflected in the use of protocols?

Home Groups

A *Home Group* is a group of two to four students who work closely together. *Home Groups* are usually designated by the teacher, creating groups of learners who would work well with each other. Over time, students can learn how to develop strong work teams and make suggestions for *Home Groups*. Students in a *Home Group* tackle some projects together; however, each must work independently to build content mastery, so each member can contribute to group brainstorming sessions and conversations. Additionally, *Home Group* members turn to one another first when they have questions about process, directions, and resources (not necessarily about academics). *Home Groups* contribute to the **culture of social and emotional learning**. Where you are using problem- or project-based learning tasks, the *Home Groups* would remain intact through the unit; otherwise, you might keep them together for three to five weeks so that they build collaborative work skills as a team.

Groups are heterogeneously formed. At the lowest levels, a buddy is a good start, thus, a group of two. As first-grade students become more accustomed to working with someone else as a learning partner, expand the size to three. At Grade 4, introduce groups of four, requiring students to schedule their use of time taking all group members into account, engage in conversations where all students have opportunities to contribute, and reach consensus rather than vote. If students are having difficulty engaging as a group of four, consider making the next set of *Home Groups* smaller. Even at the high school level, however, keep group size to no more than four, as it is easier for students to interact well with others in small groups.

At the start of a school year, or the start of using *Home Groups*, begin with some short, fun group challenges so that students learn to work as a team. Have them share ideas and instruct one student (the builder) to build the tallest free-standing structure that can support a small bag of candy or other object using only straws and paper clips. Have them develop a group name using consensus strategies so that, in the end, all students like or can live with the choice. With social distancing in place, use online apps that allow students to manipulate objects as a team or have students work in a cloud-based document as a team to produce a solution to a challenge. Essentially, engage students in work that is not content-related and pressure-filled as they learn to follow protocols (expectations for engaging with one another or completing a certain type of activity) and norms (expectations for work habits and working as part of a larger learning community).

If your students are all working remotely, establish times for them to work in a virtual room together on videoconference, with adult supervision from you, a co-teacher, or a teaching assistant. The role of the adult is to observe, be in the room, and provide feedback, insights, or resources as seems appropriate. If your students are attending school in a hybrid fashion, it may be best to keep your *Home Group* members together, that is, all at home or all in school. If your school allows students to engage in meeting rooms without direct adult supervision, then a mix of two students in school and two at home could work well, particularly since the teacher *is* in the classroom supervising the students who are connecting with others at home.

As you develop structures to position students for success in independent and group work, you'll want to consider what structures you can use to help them visualize what quality work would look like in your opinion. A *Quality Work Board* can provide that look into your mind's expectations.

STOP! Turn to Your *Efficacy Notebook*

Reflect on this section on *Home Groups* to position students for success in collaborative learning. Then, answer the following questions in your digital or paper *Efficacy Notebook*.

1 What makes a *Home Group* different from creating groups to engage in various activities?
2 In what ways can you use *Home Groups* to better position students to achieve success?
3 What kind of protocols might you develop to increase the success of your *Home Groups*?

Quality Work Board

It sometimes helps for students to have a visual that represents your expectations, beyond the printed *Analytic Rubric*. Create a digital *Quality Work Board* where you post exemplars: examples of excellent work. If your projects and assignments are open-ended, you won't be posting answers; you should not be positioning students to copy but, rather, to be inspired.

A sixth-grade ELA teacher presented her students with the challenge of writing a modern-day myth around a product or team that bears a mythological name. As an example, she wrote a myth on "How the Honda Odyssey Got Its Name." She created this story about how Odysseus was called from Ithaca to head to New York City to help fight crime. He borrowed a neighbor's SUV and headed out. Along the way, he picked up Zeus, who kept banging his head on the car roof. You get the picture. The end of the story had Odysseus recommending to Honda some modifications, such as more headroom, to their new model, the Odyssey. And that's how the Honda Odyssey got its name! Or so goes the myth. The teacher reported that her students loved her humorous myth that accurately depicted events from the mythology they'd been studying, and she ended up getting some of the best writing she'd seen yet out of them.

There is great value to a *Quality Work Board* for positioning students for success. Avoid posting current students' work. You don't want students feeling badly that their work is not shown, and you don't want students working only to have their work posted. Instead, collect work to post for a future class, with names withheld, and create your own entries. Clearly, the *Quality Work Board* works best when projects are open-ended. If the task is to create the shortest route from the school to the post office, there is only one answer, so to post the work would be to give away the answer. As you can see from the example of the myth, however, you can highlight quality components and still allow students to build their own solutions.

All of these structures help position students for success individually and as a team member, related to academics and social interaction. How might you introduce students to them?

The *Priming Plan*

In his book *Blink*, Malcolm Gladwell shared a 1996 NYU research experiment in which college students were asked to be part of a study by taking words and combining them into sentences. Students walked down a long hallway to the room where they then built the sentences. The researchers filmed the students walking down the hallway to the room and then back out. Students walked down the hallway with ease, typical of their age. When they left the room and walked back, they walked a bit more slowly. Why? The words on the cards were those typically associated with old age, such as "wrinkles," "bingo," "Florida," "retirement," etc. As a result of working with those words, students were primed for old age and for walking more deliberately and slowly. Fascinating, perhaps? This phenomenon is called priming! And there are many more studies on the topic.

So, why not take advantage of this phenomenon to benefit you and your students toward achieving the goals ahead? A *Priming Plan* is often introduced at the start of the school year; however, if you're planning to shift the way you're teaching mid-year, begin with a *Priming Plan* as you do!

A *Priming Plan* is simply a week or two of short activities, including a variety of opportunities to interact with others individually, in pairs, small groups, and large groups. Rather than focus on new content that may be difficult, engage students in using the knowledge they already have and set the stage for the content to come, building students' prerequisite knowledge. You might include a digital scavenger hunt where students find all the structures they'll need. For example, you could ask students to find the directions for using a particular set of digital manipulatives (which would be in the *Resource Area*). When students click on the *Resource Area*, you might have an initial document or video called "_Start Here" for them to read or watch to learn about this structure. Notice the underscore. When alphabetizing lists of documents, *most* computer systems will place an underscore at the top of the list, so students will see that first.

Alternately, you might create a bingo game of information to find related to structures.

You should have students use each structure. For example, in your *Home Group*, use the "Small-Group Discussion Protocol" to discuss your favorite superheroes. Then, you might have them use the "Consensus-Building Protocol" to decide, as a group, on the most powerful superhero of all time.

Three Parts of a *Priming Plan*

1   Prime students to understand the structures you are putting in place. How will students access activities and assignments? How will they submit them to you? How will they access you, whether in a physical classroom or a remote, home-based classroom? What protocols will you have in place for students to follow for discussions, group work, and more? Throughout this book, you'll select a variety of

structures to use to reinvent your students' classroom experience, including the ones introduced in this chapter. Include activities to introduce students to all structures in your *Priming Plan*.

2   Prime students to succeed academically. Start by engaging students in short activities that will allow you to assess their skill and knowledge level relative to your content. Allow students to level-up as they do in computer games (Prensky, 2006). In a computer game, after achieving success at one level, the next level is just a bit more difficult. Provide an activity and build upon it with successive, increasingly difficult activities. For example, for art students, have them view and answer questions about a drawing in one-point perspective and the most appropriate reasons to use one-point perspective. Then, move to two-point perspective, then three, then multi-point. For students reinforcing multiplication skills, start with the facts; then, move to multiplying two-digit numbers by a one-digit number, then to two-digit by two-digit, and so forth. Completing one activity allows students to move to successive levels to demonstrate their abilities at higher and higher levels of skill mastery.

3   Prime students to believe in themselves and feel good about themselves. Engage them in selecting their personal heroes and reflecting on why they chose them. Have them celebrate all their strengths and accomplishments. Surround them with photos, quotes, stories, and examples of others who are representative of them and have accomplished great things so that they, too, are primed for great accomplishments.

As you prime students and physically create your classroom, whether in person or virtual, remember that for all your students, representation matters. Representation is one of the seven lenses of equity (more in Chapter 8). Consider the races and cultures of your students and ensure that the images and quotes you use to prime your students for success provide meaningful representation. However, be careful not to unwittingly send the wrong message. For example, hanging pictures of black and Hispanic athletes and music stars along with white authors and scientists without including those of black and Hispanic mathematicians, authors, scientists, artists, and the like sends the incorrect message that your black and Hispanic students can only aspire to be athletes and music stars. It is important to send a message to *all* your students regardless of race, cultural background, or gender that *each* of them can aspire to any heights in any profession. Prime students for success by intentionally providing your students with success stories that are representative of them.

More to Come

Throughout the book, you'll encounter even more structures to use in your **Hybrid Learning Environment** for specific reasons. As you decide what you will choose to use and what else you will add to the collection of structures, build them all into your *Priming Plan* to position students for success. This will add to the **atmosphere of continual motivation** and help ensure that all learners will have "access" to the **landscape of opportunities for rigorous learning**.

 STOP! Turn to Your *Efficacy Notebook*

Reflect on this section on *Priming Plans* to position students for success in your **Hybrid Learning Environment**. Then, address the following in your digital or paper *Efficacy Notebook*.

1 When you consider your own classroom or school, what structures do you want students to understand and use that you will include in a *Priming Plan*?

2 Other than what you read here, what ideas do you have for creating a unique *Priming Plan* that put students in charge of their own learning from the minute they log on or walk through your door on "Day 1?"

3 List the seven attributes of a **Hybrid Learning Environment** in your *Efficacy Notebook*. Next to each, add what you will include in your *Priming Plan* to bring these attributes to life in your classroom or school.

Reference

Prensky, M. (2006). *Don't bother me, mom, I'm learning*. St. Paul, MN: Paragon.

3

Positioning Students for Independent Learning

Students are capable of far more self-direction than you may think.

 Imagine!

Imagine students begin the day by logging into your Learning Management System (e.g., Google Classroom, Microsoft Teams, Schoology), reviewing any notes from you and announcements for the day, and getting started working on independent activities—that is, activities that, whether individual or collaborative, are independent of the direct involvement of the teacher. Students make choices as to how to learn based on a variety of choices that meet their learning needs. That's the power of the Activity List: *a collection of differentiated activities for your students' independent learning. It ensures that the learning continues, whether students are at home or in school, when they are not specifically meeting with you.*

Learning Counts

What counts in a "classroom" is that students learn, both academics and SEL competencies, in an equitable learning environment to promote student efficacy. So, to design a powerful **Hybrid Learning Environment**, you need to deconstruct learning and put in place structures and strategies that will support all students in learning, regardless of whether they are learning at home or at school.

Learning is produced when information enters short-term memory, where it stays for approximately 15–30 seconds (Atkinson & Shiffrin, 1971), is processed, and moves into long-term memory. However, long-term memory may last days (as in the case of cramming for a test) or a lifetime! Wouldn't you like to know that all your hard work and energy in the field of teaching produces learning for a lifetime (or close to it)? Teaching shouldn't be a profession in which the outcomes have an expiration date!

Learning is not easy; productive struggle is important. If learning comes easily, students probably aren't learning as much as confirming what they already know. Learning occurs as a result of the existence of the following five conditions:

1   *Cognitive dissonance exists*: When your brain is faced with a conundrum, such as "I don't know how to do this" or "I don't know what this means," the psychology of a human being demands that the brain must reconcile the unknown with the known and resolve the dissonance. Creating the conditions for cognitive dissonance to occur is one step teachers take to produce learning.

2   *Prerequisite schemas exist*: The brain builds new connections based on a network of existing, connected learnings (schemas) that are used to make sense of new information. As an example, if I already know how to play baseball, and someone shows me a slightly different way to hold the bat for better results, I am able to learn. If I've never played baseball and am not familiar with the sport, that learning will most likely elude me. Drawing on the work of Lev Vygotsky (1978), we know that students will be more likely to learn if this new learning is in their "proximal" zone: not too easy, not too hard, but just right based on the students' current knowledge. A student's existing schemas are heavily dependent upon experience and personal background, thus speaking to the need for culturally responsive teaching.

3   *There is a path to mastery*: While "trial and error" is certainly a path to mastery, for students in school, the more resources of different types and on different levels that are available, the more likely students are to master the content. Offer students varied ways to learn, including through text, video, hands-on activities, interactive websites, etc.; through synchronous and asynchronous engagement with the teacher; and through individual, pairs, and group work. Ensure that your paths reflect the cultural diversity of your students. Ensure

through your assignments and facilitation comments that there is, indeed, a path to mastery for *all* students.

4 *The information makes sense and has meaning*: When information makes sense (based on prior schemas) and has meaning (based on a connection to the real world), it is more likely to be held in long-term memory (Sousa, 2017). Work to introduce content with context so students can see why the content is important.

5 *The learner continually draws on that learning (continual retrieval)*: Every time the brain attempts to retrieve information, moving it from long-term to short-term memory in order to use it, long-term memory is strengthened. That's why practice, including teaching others, is important.

Teaching is about designing, or, as I like to say, curating, a set of activities that lead to learning. As a former art gallery owner, I learned that a museum or art exhibit curator considers a theme, establishes the desired user experience to be created, and then selects pieces that will accomplish the goal. The curator makes many decisions, all focused on how the viewer will experience the show. Teachers should be curators of a carefully-crafted experience that speaks to all students.

Taking into account the previous conditions for learning, the activities you select and create must be differentiated enough to ensure that *all* students learn. While most of those activities should be completed by students independent from the teacher, some of those activities should involve direct interaction with the teacher, whether through whole-group, small-group, or one-on-one instruction. All of this is possible in **hybridity** such that these activities will lead to learning whether students are at home or in school: learning anywhere, anytime.

STOP! Turn to Your *Efficacy Notebook*

Consider the five conditions covered earlier. Reflect on a recent concept or skill your students learned; think of a few students at different levels and with different overall abilities and backgrounds.

1 For each student, how do you see those five conditions evident in their learning?
2 Think of something you learned recently. How were those conditions in existence?
3 Think about a topic you are about to teach. Write down ideas for how you can ensure that *all* students experience *all* those conditions.

Five Types of Activities Toward Content Mastery

In designing activities to promote learning, teachers carefully identify or design five different types of activities: learning, practice, application, assessment, and reflection. The first, *Learning Activities*, are aimed at introducing information to short-term memory and moving it to long-term memory. The latter four activities continually draw that information back out of long-term memory into short-term memory in order to use it, thus strengthening its existence in long-term memory.

Learning Activities

Learning Activities provide students with step-by-step instruction in a single skill or concept; they provide some level of feedback. *Learning Activities* should follow some situation (e.g., a real-world problem or challenge—more on that in Chapter 4) that creates context and cognitive dissonance and, thus, builds a "felt need" to learn specific concepts, skills, or content. The *Learning Activity* could be an *Instructional Video*, instructional digital text, text-based *How-To Sheet* or *Video*, online activity, reading passage, or learning center. Essentially, it could be any type of activity that includes within it both instruction and feedback or has an additional component for feedback, in the event that feedback is not built into the *Learning Activity*. See Table 3.1.

Learning Activities should be arranged on an *Activity List* so that they allow students a path to mastery that first establishes prerequisite schemas, if needed, and then builds on that. For example, Figures 3.1, 3.2, and 3.3 offer a quick look at a section of an *Activity List* for early learning students, elementary students, and secondary students.

When selecting or designing *Learning Activities*, avoid excessive entertainment, as that detracts from the learning. Avoid sarcasm or excessive humor. "JK" (just kidding) has no place in a *Learning Activity*. I watched a middle school teacher become increasingly concerned as, over and over again, when asked how one would end up in a particular caste in ancient India, his eighth graders answered confidently, "You spin a wheel!" It turns out the video he selected for them to watch posed the question about the caste system, then had someone spinning a wheel to determine his caste, who then indicated that was a joke and went on to explain. When the brain encounters cognitive dissonance, it is looking for resolution. Often, the first answer that comes along from an authority sticks! In this case, the first answer was a lottery wheel. Additionally, understanding sarcasm is actually a skill that develops as students mature. While that development begins around age 10 (Glenwright & Pexman, 2010), it's best not to take your chances with embedding sarcasm in your academic activities.

Table 3.1 Examples of Feedback in *Learning Activities*

Learning Activity	Description	Feedback
Instructional Video	Five to 15 minutes with direct instruction and pauses for students to answer questions or solve problems	Include pauses to offer a question or problem followed by the answer and explanation
Instructional text (print or digital)	Text with optional images or graphics that introduces concepts and skills	Include sample problems with images of solutions
Instructional web page	Web page with information presented clearly in ordered steps to build understanding; may include clickable text, photos, graphics, audio, movies, etc.	If feedback is not provided on the web page, create a follow-up question-and-answer activity that does give feedback
Informational web page	Web page that includes text, images, sounds, video, etc., for students to explore a topic, as opposed to receiving ordered information	Create a follow-up question-and-answer activity to have students demonstrate understanding, with answers for self-check
How-To Sheet	Step-by-step instructions, usually after an introductory *Learning Activity*, to carry out a skill	Include images or a final checklist for students to self-check
How-To Video	Step-by-step verbal instructions with visual demonstration, usually after an introductory *Learning Activity*, to carry out a skill	Include pauses to have students follow directions and match outcomes against the video
Interactive web page	Web page that allows students to enter information and immediately see the outcome as they explore and learn	If feedback is not provided on the web page, create a follow-up question-and-answer activity that does give feedback
Reading passage	Offers text-based information on a concept or curricular topic (could have an audio option to listen)	Create a follow-up question-and-answer activity to have students demonstrate understanding, with answers for self-check

(Continued)

Table 3.1 (Continued)

Learning Activity	Description	Feedback
Learning center	"Hands-on" engagement with a concept or skill (e.g., math manipulatives, sentence strips, molecular models); materials are either personal to the student or shared as digital materials	Create a follow-up assignment with visuals or text-based answers

Math: Counting by 10s			
Type	Activity	Complete ✔	How do I feel after completing this? ☺ 😐 ☹
Choose one	Let's Count by **10** / Skip Count with Buddy!		
Required	Skip counting by 10		
Optional	Practice with a friend		

Figure 3.1 *Activity List* Excerpt: Early Learning Grades

Keep in mind that *Learning Activities* are an alternative to live, direct instruction by the teacher. Live, *Small-Group Mini-Lessons* will be available for students who need them, but many students will be able to follow along with a video, web page, or text without you, especially if you are the one recording videos with your own voice, as opposed to students watching one found online. As you search for or design your own *Learning Activities*, ask yourself if students could learn from this if they had no prior instruction in the skill or concept. If you find a *Learning Activity* that you really want all students to complete before all others, you simply add a "Required First" to it and place

	Description (I = Individual, P = Paired, G = Group)	Estimated Time
	ELA: Introduction — Hooking Readers	
Required *Learning*	**What's in a Hook?** Before you begin, watch this benchmark video on the importance of hooking your readers.	
Choice Complete at Least 1 Activity *Learning*	Watch this video to learn some strategies you can use in your introduction to hook readers. Take notes in your notebook. (I)	10 min
	Read these tips that explain 4 different strategies for writing a hook as a good beginning sentence. Take notes in your notebook. (I)	10 min
	Then, try the practice exercise at the bottom of the page.	
Required *Practice*	Choose two different hook strategies you want to try. Then, write 2 different versions of your introduction. Choose the one you like the best to use for your informational piece. (I, P)	30 min
Optional *Learning*	Watch this insights video for extra support with understanding what makes a strong hook.	
Optional *Practice*	Connect with at least 2 classmates and share the introductions you wrote. Get their feedback on which introduction is stronger, and use their advice to help you make your decision on which you will use. (P, G)	15 min
Required *Application*	Apply the feedback you received from your classmates and rewrite the introduction to your narrative using the best hook strategy. Organize the first draft into your class folder.	10 min
	Math: Measuring Volume	
Required *Learning*	Watch this instructional video, which introduces the concept of volume. Then, answer the following questions: • How is volume different from length or area? • What units are used when measuring volume?	10 min
Required *Assessment*	Take this quiz to see how well you do with measuring volume. Then record your score, along with today's date, in your digital journal.	

Figure 3.2 *Activity List Excerpt: Elementary*

I = Independent, P = Partner, G = Group, WG = Whole Group		
Hydroelectric Power: The Basics		
Choose two of three (LA)	Explore water.usgs.gov to gain an understanding of how hydroelectric power works and take notes.	P	30 mins
	Watch the YouTube video "Energy 101: Hydroelectric Power" and take notes.	I	15 mins
	Read the article "Introduction to Hydroelectric Power" and take notes.	I	20 mins
Choose two of four (LA)	Read the two articles on the Three Gorges Dam of China and take notes using a double-entry journal.	I	40 mins
	Read the MoneyBox article on hydroelectric power and global warming and take notes using a double-entry journal.	I	20 mins
	Watch the YouTube video, "the Mega project of the Niagara hydroelectric power plant" and take notes. *May be chosen as homework.*	I	50 mins
	Explore the Inhabitat website on a 400-year-old abandoned open-pit mine's promise as a hydroelectric power source and take notes using a double-entry journal.	I	20 mins
Choose one of three (PA)	Run the Gold Sim online simulation of the Great Falls Hydropower Plant Project and log events and decisions.	L, P, or G	50 mins
	Run the MATLAB online simulation of hydroelectric power and log events and decisions.	L, P, or G	50 mins
	Complete the hydroelectric power challenge using the Carolina Hydroelectric Power Kit and log your decisions and outcomes. *Sign up for limited resource.*	P or G	50 mins
Required (complete four LA and one PA)	Design and conduct an experiment to demonstrate the conversion of potential to kinetic energy with falling water at various heights.	P	60 mins
Optional	Read portions of the book *Microhydro: Clean Power From Water* to locate additional, relevant information. *May be chosen as homework.*	I	30–60 mins
Environmental Impacts of Hydroelectric Power Plants		
Required	Locate, read, and take notes on at least three online sources of information on the environmental impacts of hydroelectric power plants, take notes, and then schedule to meet with your group to discuss your findings.	I / G	30 mins / 20 mins
Optional	Read portions of the book *Recovering a Lost River* by Steven Hawley to learn more about the impact of hydroelectric power on an ecosystem. *May be chosen as homework.*	I	30–60 mins

Figure 3.3 *Activity List Excerpt: Secondary*

it at the top of a section. Whenever you think, "They won't be able to know how to accomplish this on their own" or "They won't know to complete this first," just think about how you could position them for independent learning through directions and *Directions Videos* (more on that in Chapter 4).

In your directions or in any *Learning Activity* you design, reference prerequisite skills and direct the student to other *Learning Activities* first if they don't feel confident in their knowledge level. For example, if you are introducing the haiku poetry form, be sure to have available *Learning Activities* on syllabication; haiku is very difficult if you don't understand syllables! Include supports for special needs students, which may include larger and more generously spaced text, images, more stopping points, and multiple means of representing the same content (as with Universal Design for Learning by www.cast.org). For English Language Learners, include images, amplification [additional definition in brackets], etc. Note: brackets are preferred for amplification as parentheses are often part of the original text.

Students who have mastered a skill or concept may wish to design their own *How-To Sheet* or an *Instructional Video* as a resource to other students. Offer them a checklist of guidelines and let them go! Students solidify learning when they teach others, and you'll gain a collection of *Learning Activities* for your class. Just be sure to review the product before offering it to others, to ensure it is consistent with your requirements and desired level of quality. Work to provide every student with an opportunity to create a video, even if some students need more help than others. Remember, it's about an equitable opportunity to learn.

Practice Activities

After students have engaged in some *Learning Activities* to build concept or skill knowledge, *Practice Activities* provide students with opportunities to recall recently learned information and use it. Brown, Roediger, and McDaniel (2014) discuss three types of practice that, when combined, increase the power of continual retrieval:

◆ *Spaced practice* involves leaving time between *Practice Activities*. Students who practice the learning in spaced intervals over a span of days and weeks retain the learning better than those who practice repeatedly in a short space of time and then stop practicing. "A little forgetting between practice sessions can be a good thing, if it leads to more effort in practice, but you do not want so much forgetting that retrieval essentially involves relearning the material" (p. 64).

◆ *Interleaved practice* involves engaging in *Practice Activities* that address various learnings so that the practice is not repeatedly focusing on the same concept, skill, or content. "In interleaving, you don't move from a complex practice set of one topic to go to another. You switch before each practice is completed" (p. 64). This requires the learner to have to pick up where they left off, increasing the need for recall. For example, it would be better for a student to practice addition, then measurement, which might require addition skills, then back to addition, rather than persisting in only addition exercises.

◆ *Varied practice* involves practicing a skill using varied situations, such as learning to read the periodic table using the standard, spiral, and circular versions or practicing the initial "b" sound by using flashcards, actual objects, and audio-recorded words. The variation causes repeated recall of information as the brain moves from one type of practice to another.

All learning should be followed with practice, and practice in a particular skill or concept should continue well beyond the initial learning. If you use real-world problems or challenges to anchor the learning (Chapter 4), you'll find that, naturally, skills reemerge over time, which allows for a natural spiraling of the curriculum. If students are learning about polyhedra [three-dimensional geometric figures, such as cubes] and you suddenly offer practice in fractions, it will seem contrived; however, if you have a challenge for students to design an original work of art or lighting fixture from a combination of polyhedra, build in requirements that involve fractions, giving students an authentic reason to practice those skills.

Application Activities

Learning and practice, however, are not enough! It is important for students to apply new learning to various situations. Application of content to novel situations, or "novelty" (Sulla, 2015), requires understanding, which increases the likelihood of learning and long-term retention. An *Application Activity* may have students applying the learning to a larger problem or challenge. For example, after learning how to write dialogue in narrative writing, students apply that learning to write original narratives for next year's incoming students as a welcome to the grade level. They write, read one another's narratives, and offer feedback to one another. The idea is to solidify learning through application. *Application Activities* provide students with opportunities to apply learning to real-life situations and to see where the learning applies in their lives. Small wins tackling real-world problems and challenges in school build student efficacy.

Assessment Activities

With a **structure of meaningful, data-driven learning**, the responsibility for assessment should not lie solely with the teacher; the learner should play a significant role in self-assessment. This builds the SEL competency of self-awareness and has a positive impact on academic learning. *Assessment Activities* provide students with opportunities to determine the extent to which they have mastered a skill. The best activities assess mastery on several levels beyond comprehension, including connecting the learning to students' lives and applying the learning to a new situation. Students can track their progress using a *Learning Dashboard* (see Figure 3.4). Create a spreadsheet of skills as the rows, where students determine if they are just getting started learning a skill, are progressing in learning, or have mastered it (column headings).

Assessment Activities require students to exercise that all-important recall that helps solidify learning in long-term memory. Students monitor progress and set goals to either continue learning and practicing or move on to tackle a next-level skill. *Analytic Rubrics*, checklists, quality work samples, quizzes, and more can allow students to self-assess and report progress to the teacher.

These *Assessment Activities* are intended for students to self-assess; they do not replace any of the teacher's assessments. Rather, they enhance the assessment process and the **structure of meaningful, data-driven learning**. The teacher still provides formative assessments to gauge student understanding throughout a unit of study and summative assessments to gauge student achievement at the end of a unit of study (more on assessment in Chapter 7). If students fail to show mastery at the end of a unit of study, it's important to build additional *Learning, Practice, Application, Assessment*, and *Reflection Activities* into future units to ensure the student continues learning. If you simply move on to the next unit, eventually the student will lack prerequisite skills for future learning. This is, again, why I am such a proponent of the five Ps of PBL (problem-, project-, place-, profession-, and pursuit-based learning). When students engage in tackling real-world problems and challenges over a period of three to five weeks, teachers can build in a variety of skills and concepts, even varying them depending on an individual student's need (more on this in Chapter 4). If some students fail to master certain skills from an earlier unit, those skills can be embedded in the current unit, increasing the likelihood that students will build more of the curricular skills and concepts expected of them.

Reflection Activities

When students are focusing on just getting through activities so they can compliantly check them off, they are less likely to build long-term retention of learning than if they deliberately pause to reflect on the learning. Stopping

Student Name:

Grade:	Third	Just Learning	Practicing	I Got This!
ELA Literature	**Key Ideas and Details:**			
	I can ask questions about stories I'm reading			
	I can refer to the text to answer questions			
	I can retell stories from books			
	I can tell you what a fable is			
	I can retell fables			
	I can tell you what a folktale is			
	I can retell folktales			
	I can tell you what a myth is			
	I can retell myths			
	I can identify the main message of a story			
	I can explain how a story's message is built through details			
	I can name the main characters in a story			
	I can tell you some of a character's traits			
	I can tell you how a character feels			
	I can tell you what motivates a character			
	I can tell you how a character's actions contribute to a sequence of events			

Figure 3.4 Section of a *Learning Dashboard*

Craft and Structure:							
I can tell you the meaning of a word as it is used in a text							
I can tell you the meaning of a phrase as it is used in a text							
I can distinguish literal from nonliteral language							
I can refer to parts of stories when writing about a text							
I can refer to parts of stories when speaking about a text							
I can refer to dramas when writing about a text							
I can refer to dramas when speaking about a text							
I can refer to poems when writing about a text							
I can refer to poems when speaking about a text							
I can use terms such as chapter to describe how each successive part builds on earlier sections							
I can use terms such as scene to describe how each successive part builds on earlier sections							
I can use terms such as stanza to describe how each successive part builds on earlier sections							
I can distinguish my own point of view from that of the narrator							
I can distinguish my own point of view from those of the characters							
I can explain how specific aspects of a text's illustrations contribute to what is conveyed by the words in a story							
I can create a mood of a character or setting							
I can emphasize aspects of a character or setting							

Figure 3.4 (Continued)

and reflecting on content mastery allows for yet another opportunity for information recall. Students should pause to summarize what they learned, how it relates to other learning, how it can be used to solve real-world problems, how easy or difficult the learning process was, and what the student might do differently in future learning questions. Students can reflect, too, on the quality of their practice and whether they used spaced, interleaved, and varied practice in building knowledge.

I remember . . . what sedimentary, metamorphic, and igneous rocks are and can classify most. Why? Not because of a lesson, but because my teacher engaged us in becoming geologists who "found" and had to classify rocks. Whenever we would ask him "Is this talc? And it's metamorphic, right?", he would say, "I don't know; the geologist doesn't have an answer manual." It would frustrate us to no end; obviously, my classmates and I did not like cognitive dissonance: we wanted answers. What we didn't realize was the extent to which teacher Robert Guidone was forcing us to repeatedly recall information, practicing what we learned to apply it to new situations. Except for maybe a unit I taught as a fourth-grade teacher, I never had the opportunity to really use that information again, but that hasn't affected my long-term memory of it. I doubt I will ever forget it. The cognitive dissonance, the persistent recall of the attributes of each type of rock, the discussion with teammates, and the application of learning got the job done. Rest in peace, Mr. Guidone!

The *Efficacy Notebook* you're using in this book is a *Reflection Activity*. You stop, summarize, or think about what you learned, and reflect on how it relates to other content, the challenge you're tackling (designing a **Hybrid Learning Environment**), future content you'd like to learn, and more. *Reflection Activities* help to build a **culture of social and emotional learning** by supporting self-awareness.

STOP! Turn to Your *Efficacy Notebook*

In your paper or digital *Efficacy Notebook*, summarize what you just learned about the five types of instructional activities to use with students toward content mastery. Then, answer these questions.

1 Which type of instructional activities have you used regularly in your own teaching, and which new ones do you want to include that you have not been using as much?

> 2   What connections can you make between using these types of in-
>   structional activities to promote learning and the seven attributes of
>   **Hybrid Learning Environments**?
> 3   What questions do you have that you hope to have answered
>   throughout the rest of the book?

Putting It All Together

To position students to be self-directed learners, create a list of all of the different types of instructional activities you've designed or selected categorized
by topics. This is accomplished through the *Activity List*. Refer to Figures 3.1,
3.2, and 3.3 for a look at a section of an *Activity List* for primary students, elementary students, and secondary students.

The *Activity List* is not meant to become, however, a compliance list so
that students just complete activities and assignments to check them off. It is
meant to fuel continued learning, whether students are at home or in school.
Learning requires engagement! So, it's important to post more than merely
a list of required activities and assignments for all students to complete. Student choice counts! Not only does student choice support a **foundation of
student responsibility for learning**, but it contributes to an **atmosphere of
continual motivation**.

Use the *Activity List* as an opportunity to provide for differentiated instruction. This tool addresses a key component of an equitable **Hybrid Learning
Environment**: providing all students with access to the activities each needs
to learn. Your *Activity List* provides students with access to a **landscape of
opportunities for academically rigorous learning**.

Design an *Activity List* that offers students:

◆   Required Activities—Learn this skill in this way
◆   Choice Activities—Learn this skill, but you choose the way
◆   Optional Activities—If you have an interest, these will expand your
    knowledge

At the PK–1 level, the *Activity List* becomes a choice board where students
may have several skills to learn, most with two choices, represented by pictures. For example, if they are practicing the "br" blend, there might be a
sing-along video or a game. Offer a choice board grid of *Learning Activities*, so
students can take greater responsibility for their own learning. Include:

◆ Required Activities—Set apart by using a color or symbol
◆ Choice Activities—With just two ways to learn or practice the skill
◆ Optional Activities—Set apart from the others so students can choose these if their other work is completed

Consider that when students have to make decisions in advance as to how they will spend their morning or afternoon, and when they have to make a choice between two activities, they are building critical executive function skills. Note that executive function is not taught as a subject unto itself. Through carefully designed structures and strategies, you build a **climate of executive function** in which students are exercising and building these key life skills throughout the day. Starting students at the youngest age on creating their own schedule for the day builds a **foundation of student responsibility for learning,** and that strong foundation will free up your time to spend in purposeful facilitation of learning.

For Grades 2 and up, offer five to seven choices and ask students to complete two to three. (Start slowly; if you are just introducing *Activity Lists*, offer fewer choices and build up the number so students are not overwhelmed.)

As presented earlier, the *Activity List* should offer students several choices for *Learning Activities*, including reading text, watching a video, visiting a website, following a *How-To Sheet*, and, if available, engaging in a more hands-on learning center or interactive website. You can create hyperlinks to any activities that are available through the internet, so students can just click and access them.

One of the choices could be a video or screencast created by you or your colleagues. It's great when colleagues collaborate to record all the lessons and share them with one another. While recording videos sounds like a lot of work, just think of how easy next year will be when you have this collection of skill- and concept-based videos! Plus, you may find that students will return to the videos later in the school year, reducing the need for you to continually reteach past content. If you have a new student transfer into your class who needs to catch up, you have the videos!

Another option on the *Activity List* could be a live (in person or videoconference) *Small-Group Mini-Lesson* offered by you. (More on this in Chapter 5.) This is a particularly good option for students who may struggle with the content, have difficulty with the language, or lack the self-discipline to move through the activities independently. It's also a good option for advanced students who already know this content, so you can push their thinking to higher levels. Generally, students choose to attend a *Small-Group Mini-Lesson*; however, you may need to require some students to attend.

The *Learning Activities* should be differentiated, allowing students to pursue activities that are in their comfort level. Teachers are sometimes concerned that students will select activities that are too easy; and at first, they might. That's where, as part of the **network of purposeful and productive facilitation of learning,** you can view the schedules or choice lists they make and advise them on better choices. Generally, though, if students are motivated to solve an interesting problem, they *want* to learn at increasingly higher levels. If they meet with success at each step along the way, they are even more motivated to keep learning. That's why the **atmosphere of continual motivation** is an important attribute of a **Hybrid Learning Environment** that connects to the **landscape of opportunities for academically rigorous learning**.

The *Activity List* may consist of resources you locate on the web, textbook pages, videos you record, or activities you design. It should be divided into sections based on skills and concepts students need to learn to tackle a larger problem of challenge. For example, for students creating a scale drawing of the classroom in order to redesign it, you might include *Activity List* headings of: the purpose of a scale drawing, understanding ratios, building tables to solve ratio problems, setting up equations to represent ratio problems, and so forth. If students are charged with designing and creating a unique clay container for a specific purpose, your headings might include techniques for working with clay, pinch construction, coil construction, and slab construction. Under each heading, you would include a variety of ways to learn. That way, students don't need to wait for you to offer the next activity or assignment.

Having students make choices and build a personalized learning plan to achieve their goals sets the stage for you to build your **network of purposeful and productive facilitation of learning**. Any adult or peer engaging with the student can see the choices made and then ask questions or offer suggestions for advancing the learning. Once you free yourself from telling students what to do, when to do it, what they need to take out, and so forth, you open up significant time to engage in the more meaningful work of facilitation. Just know that students are capable of far more self-direction than you may think.

All the structures introduced in this chapter contribute to building the seven attributes of a **Hybrid Learning Environment**. Student choice, voice, and responsibility contribute to the **culture of social and emotional learning**. All five competencies of SEL—self-awareness, self-regulation, social awareness, relationships, and responsible decision-making—are fostered when you use these and other structures to position students for independent learning.

STOP! Turn to Your *Efficacy Notebook*

Summarize your biggest takeaway from this chapter. Then, capture any specific page numbers of quotes to which you may want to return, and answer the following questions.

1   How could an *Activity List* help you provide rigorous instructional opportunities for your students?
2   How could an *Activity List* help you provide equitable instructional opportunities so that all students can learn?
3   How could you incorporate an *Activity List* into your **Hybrid Learning Environment**?

References

Atkinson, R. C., & Shiffrin, R. M. (1971). *The control processes of short-term memory*. Stanford, CA: Institute for Mathematical Studies in the Social Sciences, Stanford University.

Brown, P. C., Roediger III, H. L., & McDaniel, M. A. (2014). *Make it stick: The science of successful learning*. Cambridge, MA: Belknap.

Glenwright, M., & Pexman, P. M. (2010, March). Development of children's ability to distinguish sarcasm and verbal irony. *Journal of Child Language*, *37*(2), 429–451. doi:10.1017/S0305000909009520. Epub 2009, June 15. PMID: 19523264.

Sousa, D. (2017). *How the brain learns* (5th ed.). Thousand Oaks, CA: Corwin.

Sulla, N. (2015). *It's not what you teach but how: Making the CCSS work for you*. New York: Routledge.

Vygotsky, L. S. (1978). *Mind and society: The development of higher psychological processes*. Cambridge, MA: Harvard University Press.

4

Fueling All Learning

Real-world problems and challenges present limitless potential for fueling students' drive, creativity, and love of learning.

 Imagine!

Imagine students are engaged in pursuing learning through independent activities chosen from their Activity List. *You can tell they are not just completing assignments compliantly; they are truly engaged and grappling with content. They are watching videos, some that you made; they are learning through web-based activities; they are joining your* Small-Group Mini-Lessons, *and more. Imagine when you meet with students, they share their* Learning Dashboards *and* Efficacy Notebooks; *they discuss the activities in which they were engaged, what they learned, and where they could apply that learning. That's the power behind the* Activity List, *giving students a "how" for learning; but these students also have the "why." They are engaged in solving real-world problems, and they are invested in their pursuit of solutions. That "why" ensures that the learning continues, whether students are at home or in school, when they are not specifically meeting with you. That's the power of the five Ps of PBL!*

The Five Ps of PBL

A good problem or challenge motivates students and *anchors* the learning. As students accomplish their curricular activities, pose questions to reflect on how this learning could help them solve the problem or tackle the challenge. Consider using the following types of anchoring PBLs (the classifications do overlap) to engage your students in learning, giving them a context through which to learn and apply that learning (see Figure 4.1):

◆ Problem-Based Task—An open-ended, real-world (or fantasy for primary grades) problem that students must solve.

◆ Project-Based Task—Same as a problem-based task but not focused on a problem as much as a challenge, such as a desire to paint a still life, celebrate a hero, or develop a video to convince others of your position on an issue.

◆ Place-Based Task—Same as a problem- or project-based task but related to a specific area, for example, the classroom, home, town or city, state, country, world, or outer space.

◆ Profession-Based Task—A problem- or project-based task that focuses on a particular career.

◆ Pursuit-Based Task—A problem- or project-based task that focuses on a student's interest. Any of the previous tasks would fit; however, the key is for the student to either identify or select the problem or challenge to pursue.

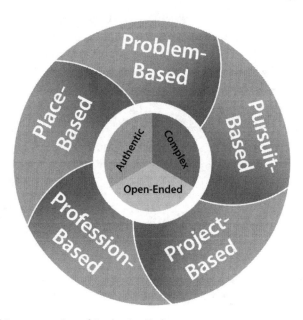

Figure 4.1 Graphical Representation of Anchoring Tasks

Anchoring the Learning Through PBL

As mentioned in Chapter 1, it is important to ensure that students in a **Hybrid Learning Environment** are driven by intrinsic motivation and engagement, not compliance. People do not generally, outside of school, tackle learning a skill just because it's Tuesday! Instead, they are driven to learn based on a purpose, autonomy, and a sense that they can master the particular skill or concept (Pink, 2009). This drive based on purpose, mastery, and autonomy is why computer games are so compelling. Games have a context to provide the reason you are attempting to beat levels; you play when you want and for how long you want; you make your own decisions about strategy, and each time you succeed at a level, the next level is just slightly more difficult, challenging you to figure it out while still seeming within reach.

Purpose counts! People learn best when information makes sense and has meaning (Sousa, 2017). Context counts! While this is important in a brick-and-mortar classroom, it becomes even more important in a **Hybrid Learning Environment**, where you need students to be continually motivated, or driven, no matter where and when they are learning.

The challenge is that to create a context for learning, you must "back up" and take a longer view. You must envision your curriculum over a period of three to five weeks (three for younger students with a shift to five weeks by, say, fifth grade) and decide what students could accomplish if they mastered the content. What compelling, real-world problem could they solve? What compelling, real-world challenge could they tackle? Then, launch the unit with that challenge! A real-world problem or challenge contributes to the **atmosphere of continual motivation**, particularly if students have had some part in identifying it. Here are just a few examples of the real-world problems or challenges that teachers can provide or students can identify to drive learning, from a variety of grade levels and content areas:

1 Celebrate someone in your life by creating a collage of items that spell out the person's name with the collage letters being constructed out of items with the beginning sounds of each of those letters.
2 Start a campaign to reduce dependency on plastics that end up littering the ocean.
3 Design an ad to convince people to move to your town.
4 Develop a "Profile of a ____," using a profession of your choice, going beyond the resume to the types of social and emotional skills someone would need to succeed in the profession.
5 Write a modern-day myth about a topic that matters to teens in order to make a point.

6 Design a garden to provide food for five people throughout the entire year.

7 Create a plan for a country under colonial rule to become an independent nation.

8 Write an original jingle for a product you like, and pitch it to the company.

9 Develop a plan for managing your digital shadow.

10 Design and cook an original, healthy food dish.

11 Build a prototype of a product that can help disabled people in their everyday lives.

12 Create a zoo habitat to house all the Beanie Boos (® of Ty Inc.).

13 Adopt a local restaurant, and design a flyer to help them attract more business.

14 Draw a still life from items in your home that represent you.

15 Create a scale drawing to redesign our classroom for the most efficient and productive use of space.

16 Develop a portfolio to address a profession of interest to you to use when applying to college or for a job.

Table 4.1 offers each of the PBL tasks listed here along with the classifications into which of the five PBLs they fit. You'll notice a column for pursuit-based tasks is not included. Essentially, any of these tasks could be pursuit-based; it just means that the students, as opposed to the teachers, identify the tasks. You could argue that some of these tasks belong in different categories, and that's fine, too. All tasks are either problem- or project-based. Project-based tasks stem from a desire to create and design to enhance the world. They may include an invention, original piece of art or music, campaign to build support for a cause, design for a biodome to support life on Mars, and so forth. Problem-based tasks stem from a desire to develop solutions to real-world problems that need to be addressed, such as local pollution, saving a species from extinction, noise level in the cafeteria, and so forth. Almost every task could be classified as career-based; the question would be if that was the main focus of the task for the student. This gives you an idea, however, of the various types of tasks you can develop for or with your students, ultimately having students generate tasks of interest to correspond with certain curricular topics.

The Case for Collaboration

Problem-, project-, and place-based tasks are particularly powerful hybrid learning structures when students work in groups of three or four. Students meet as a group (which could be in the physical classroom or online)

Table 4.1 PBL Tasks and Suggested Classifications

	Problem	Project	Place	Profession
Create a celebration of someone in your life by creating a collage of items that spell out the person's name with the beginning sounds of each of those letters.		✓		
Start a campaign to reduce dependency on plastics that end up littering the ocean.	✓		✓	✓
Design an ad to convince people to move to your town.	✓		✓	✓
Develop a "Profile of a ____," using a profession of your choice, going beyond the resume to the types of social and emotional skills someone would need to succeed in the profession.		✓		✓
Write a modern-day myth about a topic that matters to teens in order to make a point.		✓		
Design a garden to provide food for five people throughout the entire year.	✓			
Create a plan for a country under colonial rule to become an independent nation.	✓		✓	
Write an original jingle for a product you like, and pitch it to the company.		✓		✓
Develop a plan for managing your digital shadow.	✓			
Design and cook an original, healthy food dish.		✓		✓
Build a prototype of a product that can help disabled people in their everyday lives.	✓			
Create a zoo habitat to house all the Beanie Boos (® of Ty Inc.).	✓			

(Continued)

Table 4.1 (Continued)

	Problem	Project	Place	Profession
Adopt a local restaurant, and design a flyer to help them attract more business.	✓		✓	
Draw a still life from items in your home that represent you.		✓		✓
Create a scale drawing to redesign our classroom for the most efficient and productive use of space.	✓		✓	
Develop a portfolio to address a profession of interest to you to use when applying to college or for a job.		✓		✓

to devise a plan of action, share ideas, sift through possible solutions, and offer feedback. Independently, they work to gain content mastery of the skills and concepts they'll need to address the problem or project. The collaborative nature contributes to the **atmosphere of continual motivation** and a **culture of social and emotional learning**. While profession- and pursuit-based tasks tend to be a more independent venture, students could become collaborative partners weighing in on one another's problems or challenges. Students who have similar interests may wish to collaborate. One approach to pursuit-based tasks is to allow students to brainstorm and identify problems and challenges they would like to tackle and then share the ideas with the class to see if pairs or triads would like to collaborate on similar ideas.

Using Multiple PBL Tasks

Teachers may want to use one PBL task per course at the secondary level, creating multi-disciplinary tasks where possible or inviting students to use them as resources on other courses' PBL tasks that address the subject matter. A student who is engaged in a science PBL may need to create an argumentative essay, for example, about the rise in sea level and whether or not people can do anything about it. The English teacher might be able to enhance the student's learning of argumentative writing by addressing that content through the science problem. Now, the focus of science class is on the development of a science-based solution or argument, and the study of English class is on advocating for your position.

At the elementary level, teachers typically use two PBL tasks that, combined, address all the curricular content, as it is very difficult to capture effectively all the content in one problem or challenge. For example, one PBL task might have students deciding on the pros, cons, and recommendations for today's space race while using the real-world experience of Westward Expansion. A second PBL task might have students advocating for math as a universal language by exploring the parallels between the usage of math terms and descriptive language in novels. If you stay true to *always* anchoring learning with a problem or project, as opposed to having "PBL time," and you only engage students in one PBL task for the entire day, students may get bored of addressing just one problem. Two PBL tasks allow students to shift and expand their thinking from one to the next, even if all the subjects are addressed in both.

If students are collaboratively engaged in one or two PBL tasks designated for the class, they could also select a pursuit-based task in which to engage independently or with one to three other peers who share the interest. For example, students might want to develop toys and games for a children's hospital, write and produce a play to speak out against bullying, solve the school's littering problem, and so forth. This could add to the **atmosphere of continual motivation**, particularly when students are working from home. The expectations, however, must include tying the problem or challenge back to the course curriculum.

I remember . . . as a second-year teacher, I was teaching middle school students who had not passed the state tests. My attempts at offering lessons from the textbook fell short as students rarely brought books, paper, or pencils to class. One day, I asked them to tell me what I needed to do to get them to participate in learning math. We decided to engage in solving real-world problems through math. The class changed overnight. Students were excited to come to class, started bringing their textbooks, and engaged individually and collaboratively in tackling problems. In the end, all but one of my students passed the state test. My students even outperformed the general education population in percentages, and I never "got to" that chapter. My principal was incredulous but impressed. After that, he used to bring visitors to the school by my classroom, look in, and say, "We're not sure what she does in there, but the test scores are good." I miss you, Lloyd Woodcock!

Clearly Articulated Expectations

Students in a **Hybrid Learning Environment** need to be able to access the teacher's expectations, whether in class or at home. Students want to know

> **STOP! Turn to Your *Efficacy Notebook***
>
> In a "newspaper headline"—as if you were writing an article about this section and identified the headline for it—summarize your biggest takeaway. Then, capture any specific page numbers of quotes to which you may want to return, and answer the following questions.
>
> 1 In what specific ways could using an anchoring problem help students stay focused, motivated, and content driven when working at home or in school?
> 2 What possible problems or projects can you brainstorm to address an upcoming curricular unit? Generate a list in your *Efficacy Notebook*.
> 3 How comfortable are you with the idea of students identifying their own problems and challenges while you help them tie those to the curriculum?

what is expected of them; it helps contribute to the **atmosphere of continual motivation**. It also contributes to creating a **landscape of opportunities for academically rigorous learning** because students know what they need to learn up front and can take advantage of all that you make available to them on the path to mastery. In Chapter 2, you explored the use of a *Great Hybrid Learner Rubric* for work habit and behavioral expectations; now you'll expand that concept to academic expectations.

Use *Analytic Rubrics* to guide learning by setting academic expectations for students. Rather than focusing on the *Analytic Rubric* as an assessment tool, consider it to be "your voice"—sharing with students what you believe are increasingly masterful levels of performance. It's important to have students working to fulfill clearly articulated expectations. Without that, students will work to what *they* think is an appropriate quality, but that may not be what you had in mind. The more students know the expectations up front, the better. *Analytic Rubrics* are an important part of the **structure of meaningful, data-driven learning**. See Figures 4.2, 4.3, and 4.4 for examples.

Develop related checklists, bulleted lists of expectations, recorded descriptions of quality work, quality work samples, and more. The important aspect is to ensure students know what is expected of them and what you think quality work looks like. Using an *Analytic Rubric* to guide one's work efforts contributes to the **climate of executive function**. Rather than being told what to do and when to do it, the student has to look at the *Analytic Rubric* in light of work completed in order to assess and set goals, catch and correct errors,

	I Am Working On It	I Did It!	I Did It And...
Food list	I wrote a list of foods we can collect.	**I wrote a list of at least ten different foods we can collect.** ☐ **I did it!** **I chose foods that will not spoil over the next month.** ☐ **I did it!**	I made sure my foods are healthy.
Food list categories	I put each of the foods I listed in the correct food plate category.	**I put each of the foods I listed in the correct food plate category.** ☐ **I did it!** **I used my list to create a sample meal using the food plate.** ☐ **I did it!**	I identified foods that fell into more than one category on my food plate.
My opinion	I wrote a sentence about why people should donate to help us collect the foods on our food list.	**I wrote at least two sentences about why people should donate to help us collect the foods on our food list.** ☐ **I did it!**	I explained why the different types of food are important.

Figure 4.2 Sample *Analytic Rubric* Section for PK–1 Students

	Novice	Apprentice	Practitioner	Expert
Narrative format	includes: ☐ introduction of setting (place) and one character ☐ three or more events in a logical sequence introduced with transitional words *or* phrases ☐ description of each event ☐ one speaking character ☐ conclusion	includes: ☐ introduction of setting (place) and two or more characters ☐ three or more events in a logical sequence introduced with transitional words *and* phrases ☐ description of each event using sensory details ☐ dialogue between characters ☐ logical conclusion to story	includes: ☐ introduction of setting (time and place) and two or more characters ☐ four or more events in a logical sequence introduced with transitional words *and* phrases ☐ rich description of each event using sensory details ☐ two or more instances of dialogue between characters ☐ logical, satisfying conclusion to story	all of *Practitioner* plus: includes appropriate pacing and length for audience age
Narrative content	includes: ☐ problem in which character must decide between right and wrong ☐ solution to problem	includes: ☐ problem in which character must decide between right and wrong ☐ solution to problem ☐ character reflection on how he/she decided right from wrong	includes: ☐ problem in which character must decide between right and wrong ☐ solution to problem ☐ character reflection on how he/she decided right from wrong ☐ connection between self-confidence and standing up for what you believe is right	all of *Practitioner* plus: includes a lesson or moral at end of story
Grammar	includes correct use of relative pronouns	includes correct use of: ☐ relative pronouns ☐ relative adverbs	includes correct use of: ☐ relative pronouns ☐ relative adverbs ☐ prepositional phrases	all of *Practitioner* plus: maintains consistent verb tense throughout

Figure 4.3 Sample *Analytic Rubric* Section for Grade 2–5 Students

create mental models, plan, and use many other executive function skills in addition to these.

Whatever structure you choose, your expectations should refer to the final product students are handing in: the anchoring task. These expectations

		Novice	Apprentice	Practitioner	Expert
Mathematical Analysis	**Previous and current analyses**	☐ 2 plots of population data from chosen nation	☐ 2 plots of population data from chosen nation ☐ each plot contains appropriate trend lines	☐ 3 plots of population data from chosen nation ☐ one plot with line of best fit and associated linear equation ☐ one plot with a quadratic trend line and associated quadratic equation ☐ one plot with an exponential trend line and associated exponential equation ☐ interpretation of each function in terms of the situation they model	all of *Practitioner* plus statistical analysis of which of the three models is most accurate
	Future projections	☐ states future population projections with comparison to government projections	☐ supports, with mathematical evidence, future population projections with comparison to government projections	☐ future population projections based on population data plots ☐ comparison of your projections to government projections ☐ summarizes and provides mathematical model for factors that attribute to population growth	all of *Practitioner* plus provides simulation of projected population growth
Research and Support	**History content**	☐ brief summary of Malthus's theory of population	☐ brief summary of Malthus's theory of population ☐ another source on population control supporting your position ☐ identifies the effects of overpopulation	☐ brief summary of Malthus's theory of population ☐ another source on population control supporting your position ☐ identifies the effects of overpopulation ☐ identifies numerous factors that contribute to overpopulation	all of *Practitioner* plus anticipates arguments of opposing views
	Proposal	☐ statement of your solution to overpopulation ☐ some supporting data ☐ inclusion of graphs and graphics	☐ statement of your solution to overpopulation ☐ supporting data drawn from math and history ☐ inclusion of graphs and graphics ☐ inclusion of bibliography	☐ statement of your solution to overpopulation ☐ supporting data drawn from math and history ☐ clear, properly-labeled inclusion of graphs and equations ☐ inclusion of bibliography ☐ inclusion of 1–2 graphics or photos with appropriate captions	all of *Practitioner* plus inclusion of information from an interview with an expert on population OR submits proposal to the UN

Figure 4.4 Sample *Analytic Rubric* Section for Grade 6–12 Students

should refer to a level of quality within the PBL task. For example, the teacher might lay out expectations for notecards from the research portion of the task, a map, a timeline, a written summary of the problem that discusses those who are affected by it (empathy), a design journal, and so forth. Providing students with clearly articulated expectations builds a **foundation of student responsibility for learning** by allowing students to set goals, monitor progress, and report on their progress through the expectations.

Consider adding hyperlinks to *Analytic Rubrics* so they serve as a guide for learning. For example, if the *Analytic Rubric* states that the map includes a compass rose, create a hyperlink from the words "compass rose" to either an online resource or a digital page you created with a description, video, examples, and/or links out to a variety of learning opportunities. As the students read the *Analytic Rubrics*, they can click and learn.

STOP! Turn to Your *Efficacy Notebook*

In a "newspaper headline," summarize your biggest takeaway. Then, capture any specific page numbers of quotes to which you may want to return, and answer the following questions.

1 How have you used *Analytic Rubrics* in your work with students before, and how is this similar or different?
2 How could the *Analytic Rubric* improve academic performance in your **Hybrid Learning Environment**?
3 How might a hyperlinked *Analytic Rubric* enhance your students' learning?

An Alternative to Introducing Content Through Whole-Class Instruction

Even with PBL, the next question becomes how to introduce necessary content so that you continue to fuel students' desire to learn. There are many ways in which teachers and students will connect synchronously; providing instruction in new content to the whole class, or even half the class, is not one of them.

Let's just take as an example the need to teach students the formula: Rate × Time = Distance. For example, if you are traveling at 30 miles per hour and travel for 2 hours, you will travel 30 × 2 or 60 miles:

Rate of travel × Time of travel = Miles traveled
     30   ×   2   =   60 miles

Given any two of the three variables, you can find out the other. If you travel for 2 hours and drive 80 miles, how fast were you traveling?

Rate of travel × Time of travel = Miles traveled
     ?   ×   2   =   80 miles

The solution is found by dividing each side by the known quantity of 2 (time of travel). That leaves:

$$? \quad = \quad 40 \text{ mph}$$

Okay, now consider how you could reinvent the classroom experience to increase the likelihood students will learn and retain this content. In a **Hybrid Learning Environment**, whole-group content instruction shifts to a three-step process:

1. A teacher-made, 2- to 4-minute *Benchmark Lesson Video* to introduce the topic, why it is important to learn, where it fits in terms of what was just learned and what is yet to be learned, and how the content will relate to real life. The purpose is to inspire and motivate students to tackle the content.

2. A collection of *Learning Activities* that allow students to grapple with the content. Students select a designated number of activities to complete in order to begin learning the content. (One option here is to attend a live *Small-Group Mini-Lesson* with the teacher to receive direction instruction through an approximately 5- to 15-minute interaction with the teacher and a small number of peers.) The purpose is to allow students to engage in learning in ways that make sense for them and for their learning situation so they can later join a group discussion having some knowledge of the content.

3. A live (in person or through videoconference) *Benchmark Discussion* with the teacher and students in groups of approximately half the class. Students discuss what they learned and generate application ideas and questions. The teacher facilitates the discussion with both live interaction and a "silent discussion" shared document into which students can write comments and questions. The purpose is to solidify the learning in an environment where students are actively engaging and, if a student gets distracted and doesn't pay attention, they don't miss out on critical instruction. This will be discussed in more detail in Chapter 5.

This three-step approach creates an even more robust **landscape of opportunities for academically rigorous learning** than typically what has been used in the physical classroom. Let's look more closely at each of the two synchronous and one asynchronous components.

The *Benchmark Lesson Video*

Let's assume you are anchoring the learning of this unit through a PBL challenge, "The Ultimate Bike and Walking Tour." Students are tasked with developing a plan to raise money for a charity through this event; their job is to map out a local route and, based on uphill and downhill sections, estimate the time it will take for a leisurely, well-paced, and race approach, on bike or on foot. To complete this tour-design challenge, students would first have to map out a route. Then, they would have to identify elevations and calculate rate of change, to decide on the impact on the rider or walker. At some point in the unit, students will need to learn rate-time-distance problems. That's a benchmark!—a point in time that signifies progress toward the final product, in this case, the plan.

In a **Hybrid Learning Environment**, the *Benchmark Lesson* marks the beginning of the study of particular content, in this case, rate-time-distance problems. Through the *Benchmark Lesson*, you present the "what-why-wow," to maintain that **atmosphere of continual motivation**:

◆ What do students need to learn?
◆ Why do they need to learn it?
◆ Wow them with some facts, statistics, questions, or ideas that relate the content to real life, so they *want* to learn it.

This lesson is *not* presented live (in person or through videoconference). Instead, make a short recording (2–4 minutes), known as the *Benchmark Lesson Video*. It can be a video of you talking and writing on a whiteboard or a screencast of you recording your screen. Either way, it should include your face and your voice to capitalize on the relationship you have with your students. Address your students directly and put the learning in context. You might say, for example, "I am so impressed with the bike and walking tours that are emerging. It's now time to calculate how long it will take for a leisurely, well-paced, and race-style ride or walk. Last week, we worked on creating a table of how far you could travel if you rode at a certain speed for different numbers of hours. You learned that the rate in miles per hour at which you are traveling multiplied by the hours you travel will tell you how far you will travel. Now, we're going to tackle setting up these kinds of problems as algebraic equations and solving them. This will make it easier for you in the end." Then, show an example of the chart from the prior lesson. Next, show the algebraic equation of Rate × Time = Distance and start walking through adding in numbers for two of those amounts and placing the variable x in the other. That will give students a sense of the concept of the algebraic equation.

Include facts, statistics, or a fun idea for the wow: "You might want to add to your tour plan the challenge of beating the world's fastest animals. Can you beat a hummingbird? A cheetah? A peregrine falcon? How long would it take them to complete your course? You could offer badges for beating certain animals, though I don't think anyone will beat those three." You know students will be motivated to search for the speed of those three to see what you mean. You could offer a *Practice Activity* in which students calculate how long it would take each of these animals to complete their courses. Remember, you want students to feel like they can't wait to learn the content so they can explore all these possibilities for their tour plan.

At the end of the video, you direct students to the next step. For example, "It would probably be a good idea to watch this again. Then, look at your *Activity List* and complete the activities under 'Using Algebra to Solve Rate-Time-Distance Problems.' You'll see that one of those is an *Instructional Video* I created for you. Please be sure to complete some of the activities in time for our *Benchmark Discussion*."

Notice that you shared what they would be learning (using algebraic equations to solve rate-time-distance problems) and why they are learning it (to calculate their tour speeds, times, and distances), and you wowed them with some information about the world's fastest animal travelers to connect the learning to real life. That's it! What-why-wow!

You most likely won't need a *Benchmark Lesson Video* for every subject every day, as you probably spend several to many days on key skills. If you find yourself recording too many, consider combining skills to introduce a cluster of skills that will then have *Learning Activities* on the *Activity List*.

Note, too, that in a **Hybrid Learning Environment**, everyone watches that short *Benchmark Lesson Video*, whether they are in school or at home. That way, the same structure works as easily at home as it does in school. It may seem strange to have students in class watching a video while you are physically there, but consider this: if students are working from *Activity Lists*, most likely they will not all be engaged in the exact same activity at the exact same moment. So, it will be rare that students will all be watching the video at the same time while you are just standing there. At the secondary level, even if the *Benchmark Lesson Video* is the first activity of the day, students arrive and get settled at various times. They can begin watching as soon as they arrive and then get started on the *Activity List*. In reality, it is not nearly as strange as it might sound.

The *Benchmark Lesson Video* is not intended to present content instruction. This is not the time for differentiation. This is simply the time to point out the need for content and inspire your students. In the span of the few minutes it takes to watch the video, your students will either have their awareness triggered of something new they need to learn, or they will internally say, "I know how to figure that out," in which case they will benefit from the differentiated *Learning Activities* on the *Activity List*.

The *Activity List*

Covered in Chapter 3, the *Activity List* will provide students with some introductory learning activities on the topic. See Figure 4.5 for a sample *Activity List* related to this skill. Keeping in mind that you have not provided any in-person lesson, you want to ensure you provide differentiated *Learning Activities* for students to begin to grapple with the content.

While students will reflect on what they learned from an activity and how it will help them, you won't have students engage yet in *Practice, Application,* and *Assessment Activities* on the topic. Those will follow the third component of introducing new content: the *Benchmark Discussion.*

The *Benchmark Discussion*

Students are motivated by a PBL task; you have provided them with a short *Benchmark Lesson Video* to introduce the content, and they have engaged in some *Learning Activities* around the content. Next, you will engage students in a synchronous discussion with you, either in class or through

Using Algebra to Solve Rate-Time-Distance Problems			
Choose two of three (LA)	Watch the "Distance-Rate-Time" Math Academy video; then watch again and take notes the second time through.	I	15 mins.
	Explore the Online Math website for distance problems.	I	15 mins.
	Read the e-text "Using the Distance, Rate, and Time Formula."	I	15 mins.
Required (LA)	Watch my "Distance = Rate x Time" made easy.	I	7 mins.
Choose two of four (PA)	Explore the Online Math website for distance word problems; solve all problems.	I or P	20 mins.
	Read the e-text "Solving Rate-Time-Distance Word Problems;" solve all problems.	I or P	15 mins.
	Watch the "Using Algebra: Distance Word Problems" video; pause after each problem and solve it before continuing.	I	10 mins.
	Solve the distance word problems on our site; Use the Calculator Soup Speed Distance Time calculator to check your work. (If you work in a pair or group, solve individually and discuss together.)	I	20 mins.
Required (AsA and RA)	Head to the Math Forum Distance, Rate, and Time page with a friend. Read through and then choose two of the problems in the archives. Read and solve ... THEN, read through the solution explanation to see how you did. Write about the experience in your Efficacy Notebook.	I	30 mins.
Optional	Watch the MathbyFives video on Distance = rate * time Word Problem, system of equations. Stop after 0:23 and try to solve the problem. Then, restart the video and see how you did.	I	15-20 mins.

I = Independent, P = Partner, G = Group, WG = Whole Group, LA = Learning, PA = Practice, ApA = Application, AsA = Assessment, R = Reflection

Figure 4.5 Sample *Activity List* Section

videoconferencing. This will be covered in more depth in the next chapter, but suffice it to say, *this* is where you will solidify the learning for your students.

STOP! Turn to Your *Efficacy Notebook*

Think about the shift from whole-group instruction to this three-step approach of *Benchmark Lesson Video — Activity List — Benchmark Discussion*. Then, answer these questions.

1   How is this similar to any approach you currently take in your teaching, and how is it different?
2   What will be your biggest challenge in moving to this approach, and how will you overcome it?
3   Think about an upcoming topic you will teach. Write down your ideas for creating a *Benchmark Lesson Video* script, offering a few *Learning Activities*, and conducting a *Benchmark Discussion* with, perhaps, half of the class at a time.

Five Types of Videos

Just to recap, the *Benchmark Lesson Video* discussed in the last section is used to introduce new content from a conceptual standpoint, with the intention of having *Learning Activities* follow. It is not intended to teach the content but, rather, to introduce the concept to inspire students to tackle the various instructional activities on the *Activity List*.

Record yourself on camera talking about the new content, inspiring students, intriguing them with statistics and facts. Include images, charts, and graphs as appropriate. Keep it to 2 to 4 minutes of what-why-wow! Let students know what they are going to learn and why it's important content for them. Include a wow factor for increased motivation.

Beyond the *Benchmark Lesson Video*, there are four other types of videos that will contribute to an **atmosphere of continual motivation,** a **landscape of opportunities for rigorous learning,** and a **foundation of student responsibility for learning** as students tackle the PBL task. Each has a specific purpose and format. They position students to learn anywhere, anytime; they provide equitable access to all students because students can watch when they are able and as many times as they wish.

The *Morning Message*

In the same way that you would greet your students at the door or offer an overview of the day or class period, the *Morning Message Video* is used to launch the day or class period. (For departmentalized situations, you might want to call it the Day's Message if you do not ask students to watch it first thing in the morning.) While it may seem strange to record that, consider two things. First, at any moment, you may have students in class, at home, or a combination of both. The best structure to implement that works as well at home as it does in school is a video. Attempting to have all students connect through a videoconference at a specific time for you to start talking is filled with technical and time difficulties that will detract from the learning. Second, even in the physical classroom space, students arrive and get ready to learn at different times. Why should the one who arrives early and is ready have to wait for everyone else? Why should the one who got caught up getting to class have to miss information and begin the day or class period in an anxious state?

Whenever students are ready, they can watch the *Morning Message Video*. For students at home, they just log into your classroom website and get started. After the *Morning Message Video*, they head to the *Activity List*. For students entering a physical classroom, they get settled in and also log into your classroom website and get started. (Earbuds or headphones will be an important supply list item for students in reinvented classrooms!) Meanwhile, you might engage in some conversation with students as they enter the physical classroom. No one has to wait for anyone else. Most likely, they will all be watching the *Morning Message Video* at different times.

The exception to this idea of having students both at home and in school watch the *Morning Message Video* is in PK–1 classrooms. The *Morning Message Video* at this level really becomes a slightly longer morning meeting. Welcome students to the new day. Ask them what day of the week it is. (Trust me, they'll respond happily to the video.) Go over the calendar, the weather, and anything else you might cover in a morning meeting. Sing a song so students can sign along with you. Young learners will watch the *Morning Message Video* over and over again.

However, if you have students in the physical school building, conduct the morning meeting live for those students. Students at this age who are in the physical classroom would not easily understand why they are watching and following along to a video by the teacher while the teacher is in the classroom. Given this is a longer, interactive experience, it would also be very distracting having students answering the teacher in the video and singing along to songs.

The *Directions Video*

When developing structures and strategies that will work as well at home as they will in school, consider the home venue, as that will be slightly more challenging than having students in school. When students are in school and you give them directions, you can easily "swoop in" and clarify or redirect if necessary. You cannot do this as easily for students who are at home, especially if you are not in a live videoconference with them at the time.

If you want students to use a new graphic organizer, resource, or website, record a screencast or *Directions Video* of you walking them through the steps for using it successfully. You might create a text-based *Direction Sheet* as well. Keep your directions clear. Pause as you offer each step. Include appropriate images, particularly for your English Language Learners. The few minutes of video offering directions will save you and your students time and frustration, allowing students to focus on learning!

The *Instructional Video*

Picture that lesson you would offer to the whole class, live! To promote learning anywhere, anytime, you need to record that. Remember, there are other ways you will engage live, synchronously, with students. Consider the content you want to teach. Break it down into chunks of about 7 to 12 minutes. Five might be too few for you, but 15 might be too long for the brain to stay well engaged without much interaction.

This video doesn't have to include your face; it can simply be narrated slides; that's up to you. Here are some tips for getting started:

◆ Write out a list of the key points you want to make. Avoid using a script, as the video won't have your conversational self. The written and spoken word are different; you don't want this to sound like a reading of your work.

◆ Use a lot of images, including images where you then add an arrow, underline, circle, bold text . . . all of which you can accomplish in a slideshow.

◆ As you are talking, keep changing the image to engage the brain. Have a goal of no more than 10 seconds of narration without a change in the slide. That's because you are literally *teaching* content, not just having a discussion. As you offer a step or an insight, change the image. An *Instructional Video* should have the words and images changing continuously throughout the lesson.

◆ Allow pauses so the brain can make sense of what you just said. Speaking slowly is not about making every word deliberately slow;

it's about pausing after phrases. For example, "In 1666/during the bubonic plague/while Isaac Newton was home social distancing/ he developed his theory of gravity/motion/and optics/and he developed the foundations of calculus." Say that sentence aloud, pausing slightly at the forward slashes. After you say "in 1666," the brain builds a mental image of a time past and what life was like. It is not seeing computers, for example. When you say "during the bubonic plague," today, the listener's brain would make a connection to the COVID-19 pandemic: I know what that's like, so this happened before? "While Isaac Newton was home social distancing" seems like a long phrase, but you can say it quickly because it contains one concept. During the pause, the brain, again, might connect to modern times and think, I know what that's like, and perhaps think back to what it would be like in 1666. I hope you can see how the pauses allow the brain to build the lesson content with you.

◆ Add actual pauses in the video for students to engage with the content. You may have just walked the student through pictures of words that begin with the "t" sound. Now, you can tell your students to pause the video and see if they can find the words that begin with the letter "t," then start the video again. Offer a screen of images. When the student starts the video again, you might say, "Let's see if we found the same words! I found . . ." How will your youngest learners know how to pause and start a video? You made a *Directions Video*, didn't you? You might create an *Instructional Video* on solving equations. Include a pause to have the student solve one that you show on the screen. When they restart, they might hear, "Let's see if we both got the same answer." If you are teaching students how to create chords on a keyboard and you demonstrate how to determine the notes to hold in C minor, D minor, E minor, and F minor, you can pause to see if the student can now determine the notes to hold in G minor. This mirrors the "I do, we do, you do" approach to explicit instruction.

Instructional Videos are an important part of a **Hybrid Learning Environment** as they address equity issues that are common in remote and hybrid instructional settings. As the teacher, you can create the videos to meet the needs of all your learners, including taking into account special needs students, various cultural backgrounds, and English Language Learners. If you like, you and/or your colleagues or co-teacher can create multiple videos on the same topic for different audiences. Once a video is recorded, students can watch it over and over again, as much as they need. They can pause a video and rewind it. If a student is a little behind schedule or misses some time from school, the videos are waiting. Record videos for students who are more advanced, offering them more complex materials. Best of all, those videos will now be with you for years. You can continue to broaden your collection; and if you collaborate with others on your grade-level or subject-area team, you'll develop even more of a variety of videos.

The process of learning through video is enhanced when students are learning from their own teachers or teachers they know. While you can use videos found on the web if needed, the more of your own you create, the better. Or, if you find a teacher on the web who has great videos, create your own video introducing this year's key speakers, including yourself, colleagues who have filmed videos, and the online teachers whose videos you will use. That way, students feel part of a learning community and familiarity with these teachers. Try reaching out to those teachers online and create one video with all of you on screen introducing yourselves. As I've said before, it's not about what you've lost because of a pandemic; think of what you've gained! You can now create a virtual classroom with teachers from all over the world playing a role in your students' education.

Insights Videos

Have you ever been working with students and found yourself in a small-group or one-on-one conversation when you had an interesting thought, or answered an unexpected question, and you wanted to share that with the whole class? There is a temptation on the part of teachers to interrupt the class to share, but that is not particularly productive to the learning process, since you would be interrupting students' cognitive flow. And with students potentially splitting time between home and school, those "in the moment" insights become nearly impossible. That's the time for an *Insights Video*!

An *Insights Video* is short, typically 1 to 3 minutes. It can be just you talking, or you can enhance it with visuals. Beyond what you shared in the *Instructional Videos*, insights will make connections among topics and even subject areas, offer higher-order application, and share those "did you realize?" moments. For example, students typically learn figurative language when studying literature in elementary school. But do they realize that nonfiction writers use figurative language as well? When students are delving into informational text after having learned figurative language, pointing out how nonfiction authors use figurative language could be the topic of an *Insights Video*. When students learn the "c" sound for beginning words (often pronounced as a hard c) and then learn the "s" sound, an *Insights Video* for those who are ready could introduce how the letter "c" sometimes sounds like "s." When teaching students to swing a bat, an *Insights Video* could offer how, actually, the first part of the body to go into motion is the forward knee, which causes the hips to rotate and begins to create a forward momentum well before the bat comes around (that is, *well before* in terms of fractions of a second). It's all about the kinetic chain, which relates to what students learn in science class, and it makes for a great *Insights Video*.

The Power of the Video

Remember, don't think about how in March 2020 you lost the opportunity to address your whole class in a physical classroom: think of how you're gaining a video library that will serve your students well whether they are in a classroom or learning from home. You are gaining a venue for ensuring greater instructional equity. You are gaining the ability to refer students back to prior lessons. You are building a **landscape of opportunities for academically rigorous learning** and a **foundation of student responsibility for learning**, in addition to contributing to the rest of the seven attributes of a **Hybrid Learning Environment**.

The key to your video success will be in making the videos personalized for your students from you, with opportunities for students to pause the video and engage with content or offer up an answer, making connections to PBL tasks and other subject areas. You don't want to create the kinds of videos that have your audience falling asleep on the couch; you want the kinds that have them on the edge of their seats wanting more.

One last piece of advice on this subject: do not simply record your live lessons. You could encounter privacy issues in that you may have students' voices and faces on the video. Plus, in a live situation, you tend to talk more, repeat yourself, digress, and engage in other habits that would make the video much longer than 10 minutes or so. You have much more control over a recorded video in terms of how you want to lay out the content. Now your expertise as a content master comes into play!

STOP! Turn to Your *Efficacy Notebook*

What's the newspaper headline? If you could sum up this section in one succinct phrase, what would it be? Write it down in your *Efficacy Notebook*. Then, answer the following questions.

1 Which of the video types will you find the easiest to record and why?
2 Which of the video types will you find most difficult, and what can you do to make it easier?
3 Think of an upcoming week of school. Map out the videos you will make for students to have available for the week.

The Big Three: Learning, SEL, and Efficacy

The use of PBL contributes to the likelihood that students will develop a "felt need" to learn content and, thus, pay closer attention to instructional activities, thus advancing learning. The use of academic *Analytic Rubrics* ensures that students are aware of your expectations for their learning; you've set the bar for them to achieve. Carefully designed or selected videos provide students with inspiration, instruction, directions, and insights, all further contributing to the advancement of student learning.

The use of PBL creates a venue through which students work independently and collaboratively. They have opportunities to build self-awareness of what they know and what they need to learn to solve the problem. They build self-management skills because they have to manage a pathway to success over a period of weeks, as opposed to checking off assignments. Students manage their time and resources as they use an *Analytic Rubric* to guide their efforts and access videos as learning opportunities. Tackling real-world problems and challenges is best accomplished with some level of collaboration, leading to greater social awareness and relationship skills. Problem solving, particularly when the problem or challenge spans several weeks, draws on and builds responsible decision-making skills. All these skills represent the competencies of SEL.

Engaging students in tackling real-world problems and challenges allows them to assess the situation, make a plan, pursue learning, apply that learning, and, with the teacher's guidance and assistance, arrive at a solution. Experiences like that contribute to building student efficacy.

Real-world problems and challenges present limitless potential for fueling students' drive, creativity, and love of learning. Designing your **Hybrid Learning Environment** to leverage PBL as a motivator to fuel learning will support the big three goals of learning, SEL, and efficacy presented at the start of this book. Curating instructional activities that include video as key learning tools further supports the goals of learning, SEL, and efficacy.

Equity Matters

One equity issue in schools today is the overrepresentation of students of color in special education and low-level classes. Rather than working to build executive function and provide culturally relevant instruction, often, students are labeled and left to work on lower-level skills. As a result, students caught in this situation do not have many opportunities to engage in higher-order thinking and problem solving. When teaching through PBL, *all* students are tackling real-world problems or challenges that build their higher-order thinking and problem-solving skills *and* build a "felt need" for students to learn, thus motivating them. Additionally, teachers and students can identify problems and challenges that address issues of equity, making learning even more relevant to students' experiences. PBL is an important part of an equitable instructional program.

As mentioned earlier in the chapter, videos provide increased access to opportunities to learn. If students are unable to engage with the teacher during that one live-streamed lesson, they lose an opportunity to learn. However, if they have videos they can watch to offer inspiration, direction, instruction, and insights, and if they can watch those videos whenever they want and as many times as they want, they have a greater chance of learning. Videos contribute to an equitable learning environment.

References

Pink, D. H. (2009). *Drive: The surprising truth about what motivates us*. New York: Riverhead.

Sousa, D. (2017). *How the brain learns* (5th ed.). Thousand Oaks, CA: Corwin.

5

You're On

No computer, set of videos, or automated instructional activities will ever replace you, the teacher!

 Imagine!

Imagine learning environments in which teachers spend their day connecting with students through live, synchronous interaction: Small-Group Mini-Lessons *for those who want or need live, direct instruction from the teacher or for those who have mastered the content and are ready for a more sophisticated look at it; one-on-one and small-group facilitation to offer feedback and guidance; teacher-led discussions; student-led discussions in which teachers engage; conversations for summative assessment; and more. All students who are not engaged with the teacher are busy working from the* Activity List *on independent activities, fueled by a desire to learn. Live, synchronous, student–teacher engagement is characterized by just-in-time access to learning, higher-order thinking, both divergent and convergent approaches to content, thoughtful challenges, and more. This is your time as an educator! Sure, most of the content students need to learn is on the internet, but you—and only you—have something powerful to offer your students in a synchronous interaction, something they can't otherwise access. This is your time; you're on!*

Visualizing the Various "Voices" of the Teacher

Visualization is a powerful tool in innovation and for the mastery of new skills. To visualize, close your eyes and see yourself in the situation. What do you see? What do you hear? What are you doing? What are others doing? Athletes use visualization to improve their performance; why shouldn't teachers?

Spend a little time in this section visualizing what instruction looks like in various situations. Teachers engage with students directly—face-to-face—in a variety of ways in the teaching–learning process. As you read through the following list, stop after each and visualize what it looks like a) in the physical classroom, b) when all students are working remotely, and c) when some students are in school and some are at home. (If you would like, add your thoughts to your *Efficacy Notebook*.)

◆ Whole-class instruction
◆ Whole-class discussions
◆ Whole-class assessment
◆ Small-group instruction
◆ Small-group discussion
◆ Small-group facilitation of learning
◆ Small-group assessment
◆ One-on-one instruction
◆ One-on-one facilitation of learning
◆ One-on-one assessment
◆ Providing help

Now, let's reimagine what these face-to-face interactions could look like so they have the same high impact whether students are learning in the physical classroom or at home. Such interactions will be important for building your **network of purposeful and productive facilitation of learning** and for ensuring that you have a **landscape of opportunities for academically rigorous learning**.

The SuperPowers of Teachers

In the physical classroom, when teachers offer whole-class instruction, they possess certain "SuperPowers." Think about it: as you are teaching, you can scan the faces of your students and see when some have that furrowed-brow look of confusion, and so you elaborate on the content. You can see the look on a student's face when they suddenly make a connection, and you can call on them to share. If there is a distraction in the room, such as a bee flying in through an open window, you can pause instruction and address the situation; once the distraction is handled, you continue instruction.

When schools closed in March 2020 and students were all learning remotely, teachers attempted to offer lessons to the class through videoconferencing. Suddenly, students are reduced to postage-stamp-sized faces on a screen; in some cases, you can't even see all of the students in the class on the same screen. With videoconferencing, you can no longer easily scan those faces while you're teaching to determine if students are lost or if any have had a moment of epiphany. You most likely have all students muted to eliminate the background noise, which means you have no idea what distractions might be occurring in your students' homes. It is difficult enough for all students to follow instruction in the classroom; it is nearly impossible across a whole-class videoconference. Students may be on camera with you, but the level of instructional quality diminishes in this situation.

While, technologically, you might consider using a videoconference to simply replicate the physical classroom's face-to-face interaction when students are working remotely, it's not that simple in practice. The goal in designing a **Hybrid Learning Environment** is to ensure the same *quality* of interaction whether students are in school or at home. So, let's build some new SuperPowers!

STOP! Turn to Your *Efficacy Notebook*

Take a few minutes to visualize your experience with remote and hybrid teaching and your synchronous engagement with students. Then, answer the following questions.

1   What made it easy, effective, and manageable?
2   What were your biggest challenges?
3   Reflect on this idea of losing your teacher SuperPowers. Is this something you experienced in some form in the switch to remote/hybrid learning? And, if not, why not?

A Shift Away From Whole-Class Instruction

Moving away from whole-class instruction may require the biggest mindset shift. Most classroom learning experiences begin with the teacher presenting content to the entire class. Over the years, teachers have been encouraged to engage students more during the lesson, check for understanding, address the varying needs of students, and make the lessons shorter. Though it is still the mainstay approach in many classrooms, whole-class instruction in content is not particularly effective, even in a physical classroom. Students are not all at the same cognitive level of readiness for the lesson, so some may struggle and become frustrated, while others already know the content and are bored. The focus tends to be on delivery, with teachers feeling somehow accomplished that they "taught it." But years of students' frustration, disengagement, and declining test scores demonstrate that whole-class instruction largely does not work.

Add in the potential need to switch to fully remote learning at a moment's notice, where teachers' SuperPowers disappear, and now you've lost any influence whole-class instruction once may have had on student learning. But all is not lost! The necessary shift to **Hybrid Learning Environments** might just be the catalyst we need to reshape thinking around whole-class instruction.

Pupil Contact Time Takes on New Meaning

The good news is that pupil contact time actually becomes even more exciting in a **Hybrid Learning Environment**! Remember, this is not the time to dwell on what you've lost from teaching times past but instead to focus on the future that you're gaining! Instead of front-of-the-room performances (which you will still offer through video), you'll be engaging with students in small groups and one-on-one, where you can assess individual students' levels of understanding, offer targeted instruction, discuss students' learning successes and challenges, and guide them to greater success. It's so fascinating to be able to engage in discussions with students about the content and their thinking. I was once sitting with fifth-grade students who were studying a novel, and I asked them why they thought the author chose that particular book title. The connections they made and the ideas they shared were rich, thoughtful, and insightful. The few minutes I spent with them provided opportunities to push their thinking further. In a **Hybrid Learning Environment**, discussions and short, conversational interactions are an important part of the teacher's new SuperPowers.

The *Benchmark Discussion*

As you read in Chapter 4, the alternative to providing live, whole-class, direct instruction in the **Hybrid Learning Environment** is the three-step approach made up of the *Benchmark Lesson Video*, *Learning Activities*, and the *Benchmark Discussion*. Unlike a discussion in the conventional view of teaching, occurring *after* you teach, the *Benchmark Discussion* is the time for you to identify what students have learned independently and to solidify that learning for all.

You introduced the content in the *Benchmark Lesson Video*; then, students started grappling with the content through some *Learning Activities*, either on their own or in a *Small-Group Mini-Lesson* with you. Now, you bring a larger group together (half of the class at a time) for a *Benchmark Discussion* to solidify learning. This hybrid learning trio requires students to take steps prior to arriving at the lesson, including independently completing several *Learning Activities*, thus adding to your **foundation of student responsibility for learning**.

From an equity standpoint, you are allowing students to take the time and use the resources you've made available to build some level of knowledge prior to the discussion, which may include engaging in a *Small-Group Mini-Lesson* with you. Too often, students who do not fit the mold of the "sit and get" scholars get lost in whole-class lessons. They try to keep up, but it's sometimes difficult. With this hybrid learning trio, you have now given all students the opportunity to build knowledge in advance of the *Benchmark Discussion*, and through your *Activity List* and videos, you've given them access to those opportunities. This process of engaging in some initial learning (with access to the teacher for those who need the help and guidance) before discussions also helps increase student self-awareness and self-management—important competencies as you create a **climate of executive function** and a **culture of social and emotional learning**.

The hybrid learning three-step approach is necessary in remote learning; it also enriches the learning experience in a physical classroom. So, consider this new approach to introducing content based on the need to ensure you use the same approaches whether students are in school or at home: learning anywhere, anytime.

Logistics of the *Benchmark Discussion*

You might be tempted to conduct a live video discussion with the entire class; however, if your class size is over 20, it will be difficult to let everyone participate for any meaningful amount of time. Instead, split the class in half or thirds. If your situation is such that you have some of your students in school and some at home, you could conduct one *Benchmark Discussion* with a combination of students in both places. Alternatively, you could conduct the *Benchmark Discussion* with students who are in class and then conduct one with those who are at home. Depending on the content and schedule, you could reserve *Benchmark Discussions* for when students are in the physical classroom. While that might seem to be an easier approach, just ensure that students don't need that discussion to continue on in their learning; check in with them in other ways, perhaps through their *Efficacy Notebook* entries or other assignments. You don't want students to progress too far without you checking in to ensure their understanding. Also, you don't want to fall into the trap of holding the same *Benchmark Discussion* on different days when the group has moved beyond the point of that lesson content. Every day brings new possible questions for the *Benchmark Discussion*.

During the *Benchmark Discussion*, you might ask students to solve a problem or answer a question related to the content and then, using the polling feature of your videoconferencing platform, weigh in with their answers. You might use the chat area to have students post answers, ideas, and questions. You might unmute students who raise their digital hands to contribute to a conversation. Remember, you're not teaching as much as you're solidifying the learning. You want to ask questions and allow students to weigh in and engage in a discussion. For example, if you're studying ancient civilizations, you might ask questions, such as:

- What are the characteristics you consider when studying an ancient civilization?
- What are some advances of an ancient civilization that have had an impact on your life today?
- Which ancient civilization most mesmerizes you and why?
- Pick two ancient civilizations; how were they alike, and how were they different?
- What can we learn from studying ancient civilizations?

Using the chat area or cloud-based documents, students can engage in a somewhat silent discussion, allowing all to participate and voice their opinions. You could then call on students, based on what they are adding to the silent discussion, to unmute themselves and share more. As students build their videoconferencing discussion skills, you can tell them to unmute themselves when they wish to speak and ask all students to keep an eye on microphones to give the air time to those who are unmuting.

Even though you may run the *Benchmark Discussion* more than once, to accommodate a large group, each discussion may take a different direction, depending on students' experiences. To maximize students' understanding, you might choose to make an *Insights Video* to synthesize ideas across the groups. For example, after discussing ancient civilizations with two or three groups of students, you might create an *Insights Video* to share some key points that emerged in the discussions, such as the realization that the key to the success of a civilization is their ability to produce food, which requires a nearby water source. The richness of these *Benchmark Discussions* will be the result of the teacher's development of some new SuperPowers to replace the ones lost outside the physical classroom.

New Teacher SuperPowers for Large-Group Synchronous Instruction

Instead of teaching content through synchronous instruction, you're now providing asynchronous opportunities for students to view your lesson and engage in other related activities. When you bring students together, you want to use four new SuperPower roles to facilitate a discussion (though they don't necessarily have to be used in this order):

- *The Explorer*—Focus on divergent thinking, getting students to generate ideas and questions, for example: "How did this learning connect to past learning?" "How will you use this skill to solve the problem we have in front of us (assuming you're using a PBL or similar approach)?" "What did you like about this skill?" "How might you use this new skill in your life?" "What else does this remind you of?" "What else do you want to know?" "What other skills might be related to this that you want to learn?"
- *The Analyst*—Focus on getting students to think more deeply about the content. Often, you can do this using "What if . . . ?" questions related to the content. For example, you might question the impact of the circumstances, time, or outcome being different.
- *The Synthesizer*—Focus on solidifying the learning from the various sources—for example: "What did you learn?" "How did the different learning activities get you to a higher level of mastery?"
- *The Catalyst*—Focus on inspiring students to new challenges and ways of learning. "What was easy or hard about the activities I chose for you?" "What might you do differently next time as you prepare for our group discussion?" "What can you now do with this skill or concept?" "Next, we'll be . . ."

The fact that you have positioned students to engage in this discussion by allowing them to first grapple with the content strengthens your **structure of meaningful, data-driven learning**. In a typical instructional lesson, you do not expect students to know the content before you discuss it with them, and you can only assess their understanding of what you are presenting in the moment. The *Benchmark Discussion*, on the other hand, has you interacting with students who will already have some preliminary knowledge of the content. Given that the dominant voices in the *Benchmark Discussion* should be student voices, as opposed to the more conventional teacher-dominated lesson, you will be able to gather more assessment data that will allow you to curate further instructional activities and *Small-Group Mini-Lessons*.

Your twofold goal is to ensure that students have an accurate understanding of the content and to inspire them to continue delving into it further, particularly from an application aspect. Staying with the ancient civilizations example, have students uncover lessons we can learn from these ancient civilizations. Ask them to look to the future to think about how we will be recorded in history thousands of years from now. Remember: this is just one step of a three-step hybrid approach to delivering instruction: *Benchmark Lesson Video—Learning Activities—Benchmark Discussion*. After this, students will continue to engage in *Practice, Application, Assessment*, and *Reflection Activities*.

 STOP! Turn to Your *Efficacy Notebook*

Think about these new SuperPowers for *Benchmark Discussions* in light of some of the upcoming content you are going to teach, and answer these questions.

1 Which of the seven attributes of a **Hybrid Learning Environment** will be supported by your new SuperPowers?
2 Assuming you introduce the content through a *Benchmark Lesson Video* and students then engage in some *Learning Activities* through which they will grapple with the content, what questions can you pose in the *Benchmark Discussion*?

    a What "Explorer" questions will you ask?
    b What "Analyst" questions will you ask?
    c What "Synthesizer" questions will you ask? What comments do you want to be sure to make to solidify the learning?
    d What "Catalyst" questions will you ask to continue to fuel student learning?

The *Small-Group Mini-Lesson*

As part of your **landscape of opportunities for rigorous academic learning**, the *Small-Group Mini-Lesson* allows you to offer live, direct instruction on a skill. It's called "small" because you want to keep the group size to fewer than six students so you can target students' needs. It's called "mini" because you want to keep the time to a minimum by covering one narrow topic related to the curricular content. If other students are actively engaged in a variety of

Learning, Practice, Application, Assessment, and *Reflection Activities,* your time is freed up to offer a short, targeted lesson.

You can offer *Small-Group Mini-Lesson*s in class, through videoconferencing, and through a hybrid approach where some students in class are joined by some students at home. Here are some tips to consider:

- The lesson topic should be targeted to a single skill or concept so the teacher can address it in a short period of time and so students' brains can be focused, reducing confusion. For example, "laboratory measurements" is too broad a topic for a *Small-Group Mini-Lesson*; "reading a graduated cylinder" is a targeted skill that could be addressed in a 5- to 7-minute *Small-Group Mini-Lesson*.

- The topic should be titled to reflect the level of instruction, from an introduction to nuances and advanced uses. This way, students will end up well-placed in the session. For example, if you're offering *Small-Group Mini-Lessons* in basketball layup shots and you're offering one on "The Push-Release Style of Layup Shot" for beginners and one on "The Reverse Style of Layup Shot" for stronger players, name them just that. If you were to instead name them "Layup Magic 1" and "Layup Magic 2," for example, the titles would not let students know the exact skill instruction being offered.

- Students should sign up to join a *Small-Group Mini-Lesson*. This is a process of students self-assessing and opting in. At first, you will have to help students know which sessions they should attend; over time, though, students' "felt need" to solve the bigger problem or challenge will drive them to the lesson. Always let students know if they should attend a lesson.

- *Small-Group Mini-Lessons* should be small in size, with a maximum of six students. If more opt in, have an overflow list and offer another session. Keep in mind that having lots of students sign up for a lesson may indicate the need to have more robust *Learning Activities* on the *Activity List*. You also might want to narrow your focus on the *Small-Group Mini-Lesson* topic to address different levels, thus increasing differentiation and building the **landscape of opportunities for academically rigorous learning**. You should not be teaching the same lesson repeatedly, cycling all students through it.

- The lesson should only last 5–15 minutes. After a session, you'll need to return to facilitating the rest of your class, so you need to streamline your talking points to maximize the use of your time.

- ◆ Consider having a digital handout or *How-To Sheet* to complement the lesson; for example, how to read a graduated cylinder, which would remind students of the point you made in the session.

- ◆ If you decide to use a hybrid approach to your lesson by having some students physically present while others are connected virtually, be sure all your students can see your whiteboard or presentation. It may require a laptop and external monitor or projection.

In the event you have some of your students in class and some at home, you can have a few students in class and a few students join through videoconferencing. If social distancing is in place, in-class students would move their chairs to a designated area to join the teacher, while students at home join through the videoconference.

Small-Group Mini-Lesson Sign-Up

Optimally, students will sign up for *Small-Group Mini-Lessons* based on a "felt need" to learn a particular skill or concept and the desire to learn through direct instruction from the teacher, to complement the options on the *Activity List*. Part of your role is to help students learn how to determine whether they should attend a *Small-Group Mini-Lesson*. Sometimes, students want to attend all of them so they don't miss anything the teacher says, but that is not the best path to becoming an efficacious learner. Sometimes, students don't want to attend any of them—but that, too, is not necessarily the best path to mastery. You should consider all your students and guide them toward signing up for a *Small-Group Mini-Lesson* when you think that is the best option for them. You may require some students to attend. However, be careful not to assume that you are the only option for student learning; build a variety of ways for students to learn. Your *Small-Group Mini-Lessons* should not consist of all learners who struggle with content; they should be an option for all students.

Auditory learners will gravitate toward *Small-Group Mini-Lessons*, so this structure provides an important option for learning. As you create more interactive *Instructional Videos*, your auditory learners will have more varied opportunities to learn. Your visual and tactile learners will sign up for *Small-Group Mini-Lessons* from time to time, which is why it is important to use visuals and manipulatives in your lessons. For example, if you are teaching students noun–verb agreement in writing, you might provide students with individual packs of word cards from which they can create sentence starters.

Facilitation of Academic Learning

When students are working, individually or in small groups, you can now engage with them to facilitate learning and gather assessment data. Unlike the *Benchmark Discussion* and *Small-Group Mini-Lessons* where you have a clear content goal, facilitation requires you to assess student progress and mindset and make decisions about how to help them progress further in their learning.

One-on-One Facilitation

If you are working one-on-one with a student, your facilitative role will include observing the student, asking questions, and deciding which facilitative actions to take. For example, if a student is struggling with writing the lowercase letter "b," model doing so with directions and then allow the student to follow your lead until you're satisfied with the learning. If a student is frustrated attempting to conjugate an irregular verb in Spanish, sit and work with the student to offer steps and clarify. This could be a cue for you to offer more *Learning Activities* on the *Activity List* for other students who may be confused as well. (You'll explore facilitation strategies in hybridity in Chapter 7.) It is not typically feasible for the teacher to move from student to student offering one-on-one facilitation, as this would take the teacher away from the rest of the class for too long. However, if you feel a student's progress warrants one-on-one time, be sure to allocate a few minutes to engage with the student.

If some students are in class and some are at home, be sure to connect with students who are at home as well as those who are in class. If you have a time slot in your day set aside for extra help, digital help, or working with students when you are not the teacher of record for your in-class group of students, this could be the perfect time to reach out to your students who are working from home.

Small-Group Facilitation

A good portion of a teacher's synchronous time, whether in person or through videoconferencing, should be spent engaged in small-group facilitation. Recorded videos and instructional activities offer students the opportunity to work independently from the teacher, grappling with content. However, students do not necessarily know what they don't know, and teachers can't assume that students will be learning everything that is intended. Thus, joining a group of students at work to discuss the learning in progress can be a powerful strategy in advancing student achievement.

Students should be grouped heterogeneously as a *Home Group* so they have others to depend upon when they have a question or need clarification on directions or activities. When teachers establish *Home Groups* of three to four students, they can join them and engage with more than one student at a time. In the physical classroom, pulling up a chair and sitting at eye level is important: it indicates you are joining the group, investing in the interaction, as opposed to hovering over students for a quick check-in. Still, the time with the group should be kept to just a few minutes. In that time, the teacher can listen, ask questions about the content, pose questions to push students' thinking, offer suggestions for approach, provide direct instruction, and gather assessment data before moving on to check the *Help Board* and visit the next group. As a result of what you encounter in the group, you may decide to invite a student to a particular *Small-Group Mini-Lesson.*

In a videoconferencing situation, the teacher can establish a schedule to meet with various groups at different times. Leave time between meetings to check the *Help Board* and address any issues that may have arisen during the session. Ensure that students know they must stick to a schedule. If you ask to meet with their group at 10:05, then everyone needs to be in the videoconference call and ready at 10:05, which means they should log in a minute or two prior to that. Clearly articulated expectations will allow you to ensure that you don't lose precious instructional time waiting for students to arrive.

Just as they do in physical classrooms, small-group discussions (with four to eight students) should play an important role in a **Hybrid Learning Environment**. You may want to engage students in discussions around texts they are reading, ideas they are generating, show-and-tell, and more.

Depending on your schools' policies for student engagement with one another, you may need to promote discussions in school or in a videoconference room with adult supervision. Students in school can be connected to students at home, either through teacher-controlled breakout rooms or by connecting on their own, assuming appropriate security measures are in place to prevent outsider access.

Develop group discussion protocols (see Chapter 2) to guide students in sticking to the topic, using notes and references to support their ideas and opinions, and ensuring that everyone in the group engages. This might include using nonverbal communication tools, such as the discussion tools shown in Chapter 2, Figure 2.1. It might also include use of the chat or a shared document to capture ideas and comments.

There are a variety of reasons for having a group engage in a discussion, including these:

- ◆ Ensuring that students have an accurate understanding of content
- ◆ Allowing students to share ideas with one another
- ◆ Teaching students to listen and respond to others' ideas
- ◆ Encouraging students to generate ideas and questions regarding content they are about to learn (a "kickoff" discussion)
- ◆ Prompting students to generate ideas and questions regarding application of content they've just learned (a "synthesis" discussion)

You'll want to make sure your format and directions align with the goal. For example, if you want to ensure that students have an accurate understanding of content, you'll want to focus on your "synthesizer" SuperPower, defining or stating the skill or concept and having students discuss related ideas and application. Asking *students* to define a skill or concept can lead to a student offering up an incorrect answer, which can lead to other students presuming it is correct. For example, instead of asking students what a variable is in an equation, ask them what they need to figure out in a particular equation and then state that this unknown number is called the variable. Share, too, how if you vary that number, it changes the equation, thus the name variable. Alternatively, if you ask students what a "variable" is and someone answers that it's the first number, you may have a lot of students solidifying the wrong definition. Avoid that situation!

If you want students to respond to one another's ideas, you might include how in your protocol. For example, you might start your sentence with:

"I like how you . . ." to show agreement
"I respect your opinion; however, . . ." to show disagreement
"I like . . . and wonder if . . ." to show agreement along with a new idea

These sentence starters help students learn to listen and respond *to* another person rather than simply waiting their turn to offer their own opinion. Whatever the outcome, consider what structures you need to put in place to ensure that the discussion focuses on the goal whether your group is in class, joining through videoconference, or a combination of both.

Often, teachers actively facilitate group discussions; it's time to expand that and teach students how to engage in discussions through self-management of air time. That allows teachers to focus on gathering assessment data to drive future instructional decisions. Given a set of protocols, along with opportunities after the fact to self-assess, students can begin to manage their own discussions. The teacher can participate to clarify information and ask questions to push student thinking.

In the primary grades, teachers may need to facilitate conversations initially while they model and share how to engage in a conversation. Soon, even young students should be able to take charge of their own discussions.

Part of facilitation of a discussion is ensuring that it stays on topic and that everyone has a chance to speak. Include structures for these in your protocol. For example, a "parking lot" could be a digital document or app where students post related questions or discussions that arise that are not entirely on topic. They can store these and return to them later. A discussion group might need to establish some roles as they get started, such as a time-keeper, bird-walking manager (the person who stops the conversation from moving off topic and encourages members to use the parking lot instead), encourager (the one who directs a question or opportunity to voice an opinion to those who are not talking as much as the others), and so forth. Such roles help keep the discussion organized and focused.

Students should come to the discussion armed with notes, thoughts, and questions, which are best recorded on paper in advance. These may be in the form of a graphic organizer, double-entry journal, *Efficacy Notebook* reflections, draft essay, storyboard, and so forth. This way, part of the discussion protocol can be to have students reference the evidence, observations, and other data they have captured.

After the discussion, students should write an entry in their *Efficacy Notebooks* to record what they learned, what new insights they gleaned, what new ideas they generated as a result of the discussion, and what further questions they want to explore. Additionally, they should reflect on the discussion protocols to see how well they performed as a group member. Small-group discussions are important for building a **culture of social and emotional learning** and for providing all students with a **landscape of opportunities for academically rigorous learning**.

STOP! Turn to Your *Efficacy Notebook*

Think about the content your students are currently studying. Then, answer the following questions.

1   Around what topics or questions could you engage students in small-group discussions?
2   Logistically, how will you arrange for small-group discussions?
3   What protocols do you want to put in place to ensure student success?

Facilitation of Process

While facilitation of academic learning and facilitation of process often take place in the same session, it is important to ensure you allocate some time to focus on teaching students the process of *how* to learn, particularly when you are designing a **Hybrid Learning Environment**, which depends upon a **foundation of student responsibility for learning**.

Work to ensure that students use the define—assess—strategize approach to making decisions for their learning. As you facilitate, ask them to define their goal. What are they attempting to learn, or how are they working to apply learning? Ask them what they are learning and why. Then, ask them to share their progress. This should cause them to refer to their academic *Analytic Rubric(s)*, *Learning Dashboard*, and/or *Efficacy Notebook*. If the student has not yet achieved the goal, ask what other options for learning they will choose. If the student is demonstrating beginning understanding, ask what their next step will be. If the student demonstrates mastery, ask them what their next goal is and where they'll start.

Build students' abilities to persist in a task, be resourceful, and be resilient, important aspects of a **climate of executive function**. In addition to referencing academic *Analytic Rubrics* during facilitation, reference the *Great Hybrid Learner Rubric* to simultaneously build work habits and behavioral skills. The time you invest in helping students become independent learners will pay off as you can focus more of their time on their academic efforts.

Help!

As students work to become more resourceful in their learning, they will turn to resources beyond the teacher for help. However, at times, students will need you. This is where the digital *Help Board* becomes an important structure.

Your time is spent moving among various types of synchronous engagement: launching *Benchmark Discussions*, conducting *Small-Group Mini-Lessons*, facilitating academic learning, and facilitating process. As you move from one activity to the next as the teacher, check the digital *Help Board* to see who needs help. As you address students who need help, you'll use many of the same strategies as when you facilitate; however, in this case, the student is initiating the engagement rather than you.

Students typically have four types of requests for help:

◆ *Academic Learning Help*: In spite of other instructional activities and resources, the student wants help tackling a skill or concept. This is where you can provide direct instruction to move the student forward. You can also assess the situation to see if perhaps you need some other *Learning Activities* on the *Activity List*.

◆ *Academic Application Help*: While students may have completed *Learning Activities* and *Practice Activities* and even demonstrated understanding, they may still become stuck when applying that learning to other situations. Your guidance can help them transfer their learning to this new situation. If they are having difficulty with a task, assess whether the issue is that the student has difficulty making the transference or if, perhaps, the *Application Activity* was requiring too great a cognitive leap. For example, if students are learning about the Second Industrial Revolution (the rise of the factory and mass production) and its impact on the economy and society, asking them about the Third Industrial Revolution (dependence on technology and telecommunication) and its impact as compared to the former makes sense. Asking them to predict the impact of the Fourth Industrial Revolution on social structure may be too difficult a next step.

◆ *Process Help*: Students may be uncertain as to the best path to take in their pursuit of learning. They may be confused about the next step to take in their learning. They may want you to advise them, essentially helping them figure out *how* to learn.

◆ *Affirmation*: Sometimes students just want to show you their work and have you affirm that they are meeting your expectations. While this is a reasonable request, always ask the student to use the *Analytic Rubric* to self-assess and tell you if they feel they are meeting your expectations. You can then elaborate on any aspects, but you want to avoid having students constantly asking you if their work is okay and if this is what you want.

I remember . . . my second year in college, studying to become a secondary English teacher. A school was looking for students to work on a special project in a third-grade classroom, and I volunteered. The teacher chose to have all the students who struggled with learning in her class. Her goal was to offer them personalized support to build their success and confidence so they could move into fourth grade on grade level. She used student volunteers to add to the support team. I absolutely loved the experience and, the following year, arranged my schedule to be free to spend two to three days a week in the classroom. It felt like all we did was facilitate! We moved from group to group, student to student, providing targeted instruction and support all day long. Lengthy, front-of-the room instruction was out; facilitative instruction was the name of the game. That experience caused me to shift my major to elementary education. It gave me wonderful, positive experiences in how to run a fully differentiated learning environment. A few years later, I became a fourth-grade teacher, and my classroom housed a busy, engaged community of learners with me spending most of my time facilitating small groups and individual students. Thank you, Andrea Fechner, for making a difference in my teaching career.

Assessment

In a **Hybrid Learning Environment**, assessment, whether formative or summative, usually takes place through synchronous engagement. You meet with individuals or small groups to assess student understanding, whether in person or through videoconferencing. The synchronous aspect allows you to delve more deeply into the topic to determine why a student may not be progressing; it also allows you to ensure the work you are seeing has been completed by the students themselves. In a fully in-class situation, you can offer a more conventional paper-and-pencil test to all students at the same time. In a hybrid situation, you can use that same approach, albeit with perhaps two different forms of the test to administer on alternate days. For students in remote situations, you'll want to make sure you are watching them in the test situation. However, all this thinking is still the result of the factory model of efficiency in testing. True assessment should be ongoing and varied. Now is the time to rethink how you determine each student's level of understanding and application of the curricular concepts or skills. #DoSomethingDifferent.

Chapter 7 will address both types of assessment in detail. For now, just know that it is yet another way in which you will use your synchronous pupil contact time.

Herding Cats

What happens when you have students working remotely, out of your easy reach, and you need to connect with them? What if you can't find them? How will you get in touch with them? The idiom "It's like herding cats" seems to apply here. Being a cat lover, I have this image of cats running all over the house and me trying to gather them together. Well, that can be the reality in remote and hybrid learning. Here are some tips to help.

- Use "Breakout Rooms for One" — assign each student a videoconference room in which to work, even if they are working on an *Activity List* or offline activities. At any time, you can join their room and connect with them. This is particularly useful for the youngest learners and students with special needs. They don't have to worry about joining and rejoining meetings; they are within easy reach.
- Use a Learning Management System (e.g., Google Classroom, Microsoft Teams, Schoology) to post all synchronous meetings: *Benchmark Discussions*, other discussions, conferences, group collaboration, etc. Make it clear, introduced in your *Priming Plan* (Chapter 2), that students must be on time for these meetings, thus they should be sure to connect a minute or two early in case of technical difficulties.
- Where possible, use videos so students are not depending on synchronous connections to "sit and get" but, rather, to engage with you and others. Why join a videoconference lesson if I can learn the content from a text, video, or website? Synchronous time can be reserved for more engaging conversations.
- Be sure to cover all your expectations for synchronous engagement in your *Great Hybrid Learner Rubric* (Chapter 2).

The 5-5-5-5 Approach

As you've seen from Chapters 3, 4, and now 5, as the teacher, you will design a powerful **Hybrid Learning Environment** through a combination of:

- Five Ps of PBL
- Five types of videos
- Five types of instructional activities on an *Activity List*
- Five types of synchronous engagement for discussions, facilitation, and assessment

A motivating real-world problem or challenge sets the stage for learning by providing a "felt need" to learn. The *Morning Message, Directions Video, Benchmark Lesson Video, Instructional VIdeo,* and *Insights Video,* particularly those designed by you, combined with an *Activity List* filled with *Learning, Practice, Application, Assessment,* and *Reflection Activities,* offer students access to opportunities to learn anywhere, anytime. With those structures in place, you now have the ability to make your synchronous time count! Your interactions with students will be rich with discussion, challenging students to new heights, providing just-in-time instruction, and more.

The availability of instructional opportunities coupled with the "learn anywhere, anytime" nature of the videos and instructional activities contributes to instructional equity, the likelihood of greater learning, and students' growth in SEL. All of that combines to help position students for successful solution-finding, adding to their sense of efficacy. While all of that is necessary in the learning process, the key, however, is you! It is through your synchronous engagement with students that you will take their thinking to higher levels; you will draw out their ideas; you are the key to their success. No computer, set of videos, or automated instructional activities will ever replace you, the teacher!

 STOP! Turn to Your *Efficacy Notebook*

1 Summarize your takeaways from this chapter.
2 What short-term goals will you set for yourself as a result of reading this chapter?
3 How does content in this chapter relate to something you read in another chapter?

6

School Starts With "S" for Social

A student with all the content learning in the world who lacks the ability to interact meaningfully and productively with others leaves school with little.

 ## Imagine!

Imagine classrooms in which students move seamlessly through the day between independent learning and synchronous engagement with the teacher. They feel good about themselves, know their strengths, and set goals for continual improvement. They engage easily with one another, teachers, and parents and caregivers at home. They enjoy collaborating with their peers and receiving feedback on their accomplishments from both their peers and adults. They work through conflicts with others and know how to reach consensus when making group decisions. They enjoy the challenge of new, unfamiliar content and persist in their pursuits until they achieve success. These are students with high social and emotional learning, and school is the place that much of that is fostered.

The Social Responsibility of Schools

While much of the focus in schools over recent decades has become laser-focused on academic mastery, particularly in the areas of language and math, it is important to remember that school is where students also learn critical social and emotional learning skills. In an increasingly diverse, connected society, the quest for global citizens must be rooted in schooling.

In school, students learn to share, listen to others, wait their turn, consider multiple sides to a situation, empathize, debate, reach consensus, and more. Students learn from one another. They can, given the right learning environment, grow in respect for and appreciation of the cultural differences among classmates. Socialization is a pathway to success in life and career. It is an important reason for not placing an emphasis on live, teacher-delivered, whole-group learning, instead building a collaborative learning environment with students learning with and from one another. The teacher becomes the curator and facilitator. With technology enabling the delivery of content in numerous other ways, teachers can engage synchronously in ways that advance learning, build SEL skills, and increase efficacy.

Prior to the implementation of the efficiency-focused, factory model of schools, inspired by the Industrial Revolution, the one-room schoolhouse represented a community social structure. Students from kindergarten through eighth grade learned together in one large room. Older students helped younger students increase their own sense of efficacy; students learned to engage with those of different ages. I am not attempting to glamorize the one-room schoolhouse, as it certainly had its drawbacks; however, it is an interesting point in history. The shift away from school as a community social structure may have, as an unintended consequence, contributed to a decrease in social and emotional learning skills and an increase in mental health issues. There is more to learn in school than the three Rs: "reading, 'riting, and 'rithmetic."

The Five Competencies of SEL in Hybrid Learning

Consider the five competencies of social and emotional learning, as defined by CASEL (www.casel.org): self-awareness, self-management, social awareness, relationship skills, and responsible decision-making. How can you foster each of these in your newly reinvented classroom experience? Get your *Efficacy Notebook* ready, and make an entry after each competency. If you want to include an image in your *Efficacy Notebook*, head to www.casel.org for the SEL competencies!

Self-Awareness

How can students become aware of how their emotions and thoughts affect their behaviors? How will they build a strong sense of self and their strengths, leading to confidence? How will they build an understanding of their limitations and act in ways that acknowledge that? How will they build a strong sense of self and celebrate who they are? Here are a few structures and strategies from a **Hybrid Learning Environment** that align with the SEL competencies to give you some ideas:

- *Analytic Rubrics*, whether focused on academic performance or the *Great Hybrid Learner Rubric*, allow students to self-assess and identify where they are on a continuum in order to set realistic goals for themselves.
- Learning styles inventories allow students to gain an understanding of how they learn best and challenge themselves to broaden their ability to learn through a variety of venues.
- A *Priming Plan* can help students see themselves through their heroes, giving them hope for their own successful future. It can also give them a sense of where they excel academically and where they need to focus in the future.
- The *Efficacy Notebook* is a place where students can reflect on what and how they learn; design questions focused on building self-awareness.
- *Small-Group Mini-Lessons* allow students to identify learning needs and sign up to participate.

Self-Management

How will students learn to regulate their emotions and thoughts and resulting behaviors? How will they direct their own learning? How will they manage their emotions and reactions in stressful situations? How will they set goals and persist in their pursuit of them? Clearly, so many of the structures in your reinvented classroom experience are focused on self-management:

- The *Activity List* provides students with choice as to when and how they learn. It enables students to set goals and achieve them related to pursuing learning.
- Scheduling their own time builds in students the ability to set goals, make reasonable plans, and stick with them.
- Engaging in pairs and group activities provides students with opportunities to manage their behaviors and reactions in social situations, and, at times, to reflect on them through the *Teamwork Journal* (formerly, the *Table Journal*)—team members discuss and answer four to five questions about how they performed as a team.

◆ The *Help Board* allows students to advocate for themselves, recognizing when they are stuck and need help.

Social Awareness

How will students build empathy for others? How will they learn to see the perspective of others, particularly those from diverse backgrounds and cultures? How will they build an understanding of norms for behavior? How will they come to reach out to the network of adults in their lives for support? How will they engage as one of a diverse community of learners? Consider these structures and strategies for your **Hybrid Learning Environment**:

◆ Protocols position students for success in social situations, defining for them appropriate behaviors and actions.

◆ Problem- and project-based challenges should be designed to address social issues, equity, and diversity so students can collaboratively work to tackle real-world problems related to social engagement.

◆ *Home Groups* allow students to build skills in working with others toward a common goal.

◆ *Peer Experts* learn to see the other person's perspective and engage with them in ways that build learning.

Relationship Skills

How will students learn to work as a valued member of a group? How will they learn to listen and contribute to conversations? How will they learn to resolve conflicts that arise within the group? How will they learn to ask for and offer help when needed? How will they learn to build relationships with culturally diverse others, showing respect for cultural differences? You can help students build relationship skills through the structures and strategies you use:

◆ *Home Groups* allow students to work as a group to develop a solution to a problem, which includes collaborative brainstorming and consensus-building.

◆ Peer editing helps students play a positive role in enhancing one another's academic performance.

◆ *Peer Experts* allow students to both receive and give assistance. Often, students will look at the *Help Board* and, if they feel they can be of assistance, will offer help to the student whose name is on it.

◆ Problem- and project-based learning allows students to work with one another, through their differences, and build relationships as they work toward a common goal.

Responsible Decision-Making

How will students learn to make decisions as part of a greater community? How will they learn to act in ways that are respectful of others and contribute to the greater whole? How will they learn to make decisions that promote safety and follow social norms? How will they consider their actions in terms of consequences and unintended consequences? As you move from mere compliance to putting students in charge of their own learning, you can build a **Hybrid Learning Environment** that helps students build responsible decision-making skills. Consider using these structures and strategies:

◆ Problem- and project-based learning, when designed around situations that challenge students to consider the plight of others, allows students to employ decision-making strategies for the greater good.

◆ Students scheduling their time from a well-constructed *Activity List* provides students with opportunities to negotiate with one another to decide on times to meet to tackle pairs and group activities, requiring students to make responsible decisions.

I remember . . . taking a position teaching middle school math when I really wanted a position as an elementary school teacher. I said to the principal interviewing me that I would take the position if he promised to let me transfer to one of the elementary schools when a position opened, and he agreed. That year, he asked me to join a more veteran teacher in launching an eighth-grade musical with the goal of involving all students; I agreed. We then engaged many of the faculty members and worked with students to figure out, with them, the best roles for each student. I was responsible for teaching a group of students the Lindy Hop (a dance from the late 1930s; yes, I had to learn it myself!). What a fun year it was preparing for that, watching students engage with one another outside the academic venue. Students supported one another, shared their struggles, offered one another compliments and critiques, and exhibited so many of the skills to which we now refer as SEL. The principal wanted to build something beyond academics for these students and ensure that each of them succeeded in some way. He understood that a student with all the content learning in the world who lacks the ability to interact meaningfully and productively with others leaves school with little. I will always remember you, Ridgefield, New Jersey, Eighth-Grade Class of 1979.

> **STOP! Turn to Your *Efficacy Notebook***
> Think of how you can build a **culture of social and emotional learning** in your **Hybrid Learning Environment**. Write down your ideas for structures and strategies you will use as you answer these questions.
>
> 1 What structures or strategies do you already use for building SEL that will work as well at home as they do in school?
> 2 What additional structures or strategies may you want to incorporate to ensure students working at home are successful?

Executive Function as the Path to SEL

Just behind your forehead is the prefrontal cortex section of the brain. It is the part of the brain that handles many of the skills of executive function. Following multiple steps, seeing multiple sides to a situation, being creative, managing time, making inferences, generating possible solutions, thinking before acting, and monitoring performance are just a sampling of executive function skills. As you can see, these skills are crucial to academic achievement; they are also crucial to social and emotional learning. This is why it is so important to create a **climate of executive function** in your **Hybrid Learning Environment**, with "climate" referring to those conditions that have a widespread effect on life, activity, etc. (from yourdictionary.com). Executive function has a widespread effect on students' school life, from learning to SEL to efficacy.

This part of the brain grows from birth and experiences a significant growth spurt between ages 4 and 5. As an example, young children have difficulty delaying gratification when they want something; around age 5, they are able to reason enough to accept that they can't have that treat until after dinner, for example. This part of the brain undergoes another growth spurt at puberty but is not finished growing, and thus exhibiting higher-order reasoning skills, until age 25 in most people. While it is often easy for teachers to excuse students who have a broken arm or other physical ability that hinders learning, they don't often consider that slowed brain development could be a physiological hindrance to learning as well (Sulla, 2018).

In my book *Building Executive Function: The Missing Link to Student Achievement* (2018), I classified 40 executive function skills by the life categories they support: conscious control, engagement, collaboration, empowerment, efficacy, and leadership (which encompasses all of the skills). Let me also point out the SEL competencies these skills support in Tables 6.1–6.5. These are the executive function skills most needed to succeed in building SEL competencies, though you could easily argue for or against the inclusion of most of these. The intent is to demonstrate just how intertwined executive function and SEL are and to build awareness of the executive function skills that you can support in your classroom.

 STOP! Turn to Your *Efficacy Notebook*

Look at Tables 6.1–6.5 of executive function skills and the SEL they support. Then, answer these questions.

1   What ideas do you have or conclusions do you draw when you look at these tables?
2   As you look at the executive function skills listed in the first column, you probably reinforce a lot of them through activities, structures, and facilitation strategies. Which top three do you feel you want to focus on more for all your students?
3   How can you build a greater emphasis on those into your activities, structures, and facilitation strategies?

Many of the structures of your reinvented classroom experience will support your students' growth in the areas of executive function and SEL. Following are additional strategies for building executive function skills that will support academic success and SEL.

Graphic Organizers

Graphic organizers are powerful tools for building executive function and SEL while tackling content. The visual cues of boxes, concentric circles, intersecting circles, lines and arrows, and more build concepts as students enter content. Whether students are working in school or from home, graphic organizers will help students organize content and their thoughts, and students can use printed or digital versions.

Cause and Effect

Identifying cause-and-effect relationships is an executive function skill that supports all five SEL competencies. While it is a skill that teachers address

Table 6.1 The Executive Function Skills of Conscious Control

	Self-Awareness	Self-Management	Social Awareness	Relationship Skills	Responsible Decision-Making
Storing and manipulating visual and verbal information	x	x	x	x	x
Remembering details	x	x	x	x	x
Holding on to information while considering other information	x	x	x	x	x
Shifting focus from one event to another	x	x	x	x	x
Attending to a person or activity	x	x	x	x	x
Focusing	x	x	x	x	x
Concentrating	x	x	x	x	x
Thinking before acting		x		x	x
Managing conflicting thoughts		x		x	x

Table 6.2 The Executive Function Skills of Engagement With Content and Others

	Self-Awareness	Self-Management	Social Awareness	Relationship Skills	Responsible Decision-Making
Identifying same and different	x	x	x	x	x
Following multiple steps		x			x
Identifying cause-and-effect relationships	x	x	x	x	x
Categorizing information	x		x		x
Changing perspective			x	x	x
Thinking about multiple concepts simultaneously	x	x	x	x	x
Initiating a task	x	x	x	x	x
Persisting in a task		x	x	x	x

Table 6.3 The Executive Function Skills of Collaboration

	Self-Awareness	Self-Management	Social Awareness	Relationship Skills	Responsible Decision-Making
Seeing multiple sides to a situation	x		x	x	x
Being open to others' points of view	x		x	x	x
Maintaining social appropriateness		x	x	x	x
Overcoming temptation		x		x	x

Table 6.4 The Executive Function Skills of Empowerment

	Self-Awareness	Self-Management	Social Awareness	Relationship Skills	Responsible Decision-Making
Catching and correcting errors		x		x	x
Setting goals	x	x		x	x
Managing time		x		x	x
Self-assessing	x	x	x	x	x
Monitoring performance	x	x	x	x	x
Reflecting on goals	x	x		x	x

Table 6.5 The Executive Function Skills of Efficacy

	Self-Awareness	Self-Management	Social Awareness	Relationship Skills	Responsible Decision-Making
Being creative		x		x	x
Working toward a goal	x	x	x	x	x
Organizing actions and thoughts	x	x	x	x	x
Considering future consequences in light of current action		x		x	x
Making hypotheses, deductions, and inferences	x	x	x	x	x
Applying former approaches to new situations	x	x	x	x	x
Defining a problem	x	x	x	x	x
Analyzing	x	x	x	x	x
Creating mental images	x	x	x	x	x
Generating possible solutions	x	x	x	x	x
Anticipating	x	x	x	x	x
Predicting outcomes	x	x	x	x	x
Evaluating	x	x	x	x	x

in the early grades, it should be reinforced throughout a student's schooling, involving increasing complexity. Figure 6.1 offers a look at three graphic organizers for cause and effect at increasingly difficult levels.

You can use cause-and-effect relationships to explain the "known" as well as to predict the "unknown." That is, at the first level, you observe an event or

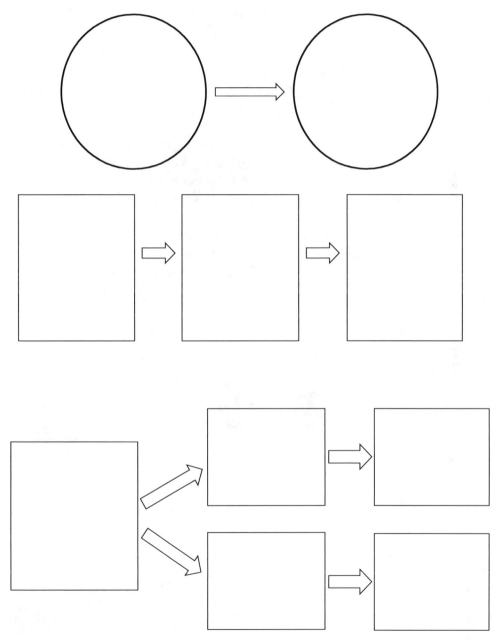

Figure 6.1 Cause-and-Effect Graphic Organizers

phenomenon, and you document the relationships. For example, rain causes soil to loosen, mix with the water, and become mud; touching a hot stove causes pain. Adding sophistication, you can identify a chain of events, such as: dust from the Sahara Desert traveling through the trade winds lands on the Caribbean coral reefs and increases nitrogen levels in the water; increased nitrogen levels cause algae growth; algae releases sugar, which causes bacteria to thrive; bacteria cause the oxygen supply to the coral to be cut off; lack of oxygen causes the death of the coral.

At the next level, students predict what might happen next. For example, rain causes soil to loosen and become mud; mud sticks to my shoes, which means my muddy shoes will mess up the floors of the house; which will cause mom to get angry. Following the plight of coral reefs, if the Caribbean coral reefs die, that would cause the demise of the world's richest biome, which would cause the fishing and tourism industries to decline, which could cause an economic collapse among Caribbean nations (see Figure 6.2). This latter chain of events is speculation, but thinking through the known cause-and-effect relationships and then predicting future relationships draws on and builds significant executive function.

You can find cause-and-effect relationships in any curricular subject at any grade level. Include cause-and-effect questions or activities in your *Activity List*. Ask cause-and-effect questions when you facilitate learning.

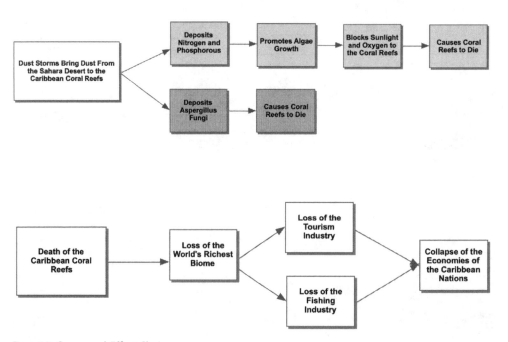

Figure 6.2 Cause-and-Effect Chain

Embedding cause-and-effect relationships into your daily **Hybrid Learning Environment** helps to create a **climate of executive function** as opposed to treating executive function as a subject to study, which it is not.

Categorization

You may think of young learners categorizing objects by shape and color, but categorization should not stop there. As with cause-and-effect relationships, categorization can be a part of any subject area across the grade levels. Have students think through and categorize characters as dynamic, static, round, flat, protagonist, antagonist, symbolic, etc. Have students categorize construction tools as simple machines to show similarity and differences in how tools help us. Have students categorize types of words, allowing them to draw conclusions about their use, before introducing parts of speech. Have students categorize fractional parts to build an understanding of equivalent fractions. Everything falls into categories! Just look at the periodic table! The more we think about categories, the more we build executive function. As with cause and effect, embedding categorization into your daily instructional activities and facilitation helps to create a **climate of executive function**.

Increasing Task Persistence

Persisting in a task is an executive function skill that supports engagement in content and navigating relationships with others; thus, it strengthens the SEL competencies of self-management, relationship skills, and making responsible decisions. Design a digital or paper form that allows students to stop and reflect when they want to quit or walk away. Have them document how they are feeling, why they are feeling that way, and what they could do about it. See Figure 6.3, from the book *Building Executive Function: The Missing Link to Student Achievement* (Sulla, 2018, p. 127).

Norms for Socialization

As you design your *Great Hybrid Learner Rubric* (presented in Chapter 2), be sure to include norms related to social engagement, ranging from showing respect for one's teacher and classmates to discussion participation to academic collaboration. Also presented in Chapter 2, protocols, or norms of

Task Persistence Card

I want to give up on _____.

I feel	Because	But I will try to...
❑ Frustrated ❑ Angry ❑ Confused ❑ Lost ❑ _____		

Figure 6.3 Task Persistence Card

engagement, position students for successful socialization and contribute to the **culture of social and emotional learning**.

In a **Hybrid Learning Environment**, students will not always be face-to-face with their classmates. As a first step to creating a collaborative learning community, have students record a 1-minute video introducing themselves to one another. Include a checklist of items to include to guide students, for example:

- ◆ Full name, carefully enunciated
- ◆ What makes you a good classmate
- ◆ Your favorite school subject
- ◆ What you aspire to be when you grow up
- ◆ What you do when you get stuck in a learning situation
- ◆ What you hope to learn more about this year

Obviously, you would create the checklist based on your students' ages and subject area. Consider how these questions relate back to executive function and SEL skills. Asking about getting stuck in a learning situation draws on the executive function skills of monitoring performance, persisting in a task, being open to others' points of view, working toward a goal, considering future consequences in light of current action, applying former approaches to new situations, and more. It draws on all the SEL competencies: self-awareness, self-management, social awareness, relationship skills, and responsible decision-making. All that out of one question! Creating opportunities and supports for students to learn successful socialization skills builds a **climate of executive function** and a **culture of social and emotional learning**.

STOP! Turn to Your *Efficacy Notebook*

Consider your **Hybrid Learning Environment** and how you plan to strengthen your **climate of executive function** and **culture of social and emotional learning**. Then, answer these questions.

1   In what ways do students typically engage with one another throughout the day? Make a list.
2   Using that list, what checklists, protocols, and other structures might you create to build stronger executive function skills and SEL competencies?

Reference

Sulla, N. (2018). *Building executive function: The missing link to student achievement*. New York: Routledge.

7

Teacher as GPS

You can't calculate how far you have to go unless you know where you're going!

 Imagine!

Imagine a learning environment where students continuously set goals based on their interests and the curricular goals set by their teacher, where students and teachers continuously partner to ensure that the students achieve those goals, and where students and teachers use a variety of instruments for continuously checking progress and supporting students toward success. Imagine a learning world in which ongoing assessment drives decision-making on the part of the student and teacher!

A Favorite Metaphor

I often talk and write about "teacher as GPS" (Sulla, 2015). Think about it! You enter a destination (your goal) into your GPS. Your GPS maps out a path for you; however, you make some decisions as to *how* you like to travel, whether on highways, toll roads, or side roads. As you travel, your GPS continually sends out satellite signals to assess your progress. If it seems you've moved off the path to your destination, your GPS will recalculate a route to get you there. Your GPS never tells you to try harder, never tells you this is the last time it'll recalculate for you, and never gives up on getting you to your destination. How wonderful a metaphor is *that* for the facilitation power of a teacher?

The teacher and students set goals. After all, you can't calculate how far you have to go unless you know where you're going! The teacher offers a pathway to success for students consisting of lessons, activities, and assignments, making decisions based on how students learn best. The teacher then continually assesses student progress and, based on that progress, offers advice, resources, and potentially alternate ways to achieve the goal.

STOP! Turn to Your *Efficacy Notebook*

Consider how this "teacher as GPS" metaphor applies to a **Hybrid Learning Environment** and answer these questions.

1   What about this metaphor mirrors the way you currently teach?
2   How can a teaching mindset based on this metaphor ensure that you have a **structure of meaningful, data-driven learning**?
3   How would a teaching mindset based on this metaphor depend upon the development of a **landscape of opportunities for academically rigorous learning**?

Tough Talk

Okay, get ready for some tough talk! Assessment is not a dirty word. Standardized assessments should not be eliminated. They should, however, cease to be viewed as an interruption in the learning process. They *are* a critical part of the learning process. Why do bakers stick toothpicks in brownies to determine if they are fully cooked? Why do cooks put thermometers in a roast while they are cooking? Why do painters lightly touch a painted surface to see if it's tacky? Why do firefighters feel a door before opening it? Why do healthcare workers take your temperature and blood pressure when you arrive at a doctor's office? Assessments, assessments, assessments! They are a valuable part of life, and they've gotten a bad reputation in schooling. Students should be assessing their progress daily; teachers should be assessing students' progress daily. Those assessments should lead to purposeful and deliberate decisions about next steps, just as they do in every other area of daily life.

Assessments should (generally) *not* be differentiated, nor should there be a need to do so. First, assessments should be geared to the goals students are tackling. It makes no sense to assess second graders on figurative language if that's not what they're learning. However, it does make sense to assess them on, say, the use of descriptive language in their writing. It does make sense to assess a sixth grader on geometric measurements. If a student has difficulty with geometric measurements, the last thing you want to do is redesign the assessment to be easier or even to match preferred learning styles. Auditory learners still need to learn to access text; visual learners still need to learn to listen and comprehend information. The outside world will not always accommodate their learning preferences. So, while students can prioritize some types of learning in their work, you need to ensure that, at times, they challenge themselves beyond their comfort level so they are prepared for any type of assessment they encounter in their lives.

My advice against differentiating assessments is predicated on the understanding, however, that the assessment is "fair." That means it is culturally aligned with students in terms of language, images, and scenarios. It means that it is accessible to students with language barriers and learning disabilities. This means the assessment may need some structural modifications, such as larger text, more white space, the ability to have text read to the student, etc. That's not differentiation in my view; that's ensuring accessibility—and that's an equity issue.

Hear me out! In the world outside school, for every goal, whether it be a sports challenge, job interview, or personal aspiration, there is a bar. Others may compete with you against that bar—and the bar doesn't change to meet the capabilities of the competitors. Consider the Olympics. There are expectations for executing a perfect dive off the 10-meter platform. The score is not adjusted to account for the diver being a little overweight, or having balance issues, or anything else. The bar is the bar. That's life! School should be the place where we prepare students to succeed throughout their lives, beyond the virtual or physical walls of the classroom.

That means, though, that teachers need to set their sights on ensuring that all students achieve at high levels. That means the one lesson or activity that works for this student may not work for that student, who requires another type of lesson or activity. Instruction and learning activities need to be differentiated to ensure that all students can achieve that bar.

If I am teaching geometric measurement—perhaps surface area and volume of polyhedra—I may have some students who pick it up quickly or who already know how to calculate these measurements. For them, I may offer more challenging geometric figures, perhaps those made up of other polyhedra. For other students who are struggling somewhat, I need to provide various ways to help them build understanding and application skills. For the students who may have never used a ruler, I have to start with reading a ruler, moving to two-dimensional figures and then on to three-dimensional figures. In the end, students all take the same test, and your role as a teacher is to ensure they all perform extremely well on it.

There Are No Struggling Learners

It is important to assess and name the current condition, not the student. There are no struggling learners; there are only those who struggle with the current content. There is a difference. The latter describes a condition, which can be corrected. The former labels a child—and there is no room for that kind of labeling in schools today.

While it is easier to say the student just didn't achieve, that does not serve the purpose of schooling. In a **Hybrid Learning Environment** where students take charge of their own learning, students can all be working on different levels. The goal for the teacher is to provide every possible, accessible opportunity for *all* students to learn at high levels. For that to work, you need a healthy respect for the assessment–facilitation relationship.

The Assessment–Facilitation Connection

While "assessment" is the means of measuring student progress, "facilitation" is the set of actions a teacher takes to ensure that all students learn at high levels. Facilitation includes offering guidance, resources, connections to others, guiding questions, and direct instruction. Facilitation and instruction go hand in hand. Facilitation without assessment is meaningless; assessment without subsequent facilitation is equally meaningless. As a teacher, you are gathering assessment data every time you look at or listen to students or their work. And while, for some, the information gathered is used to assign an adjective, category, or grade to the student, in a **Hybrid Learning Environment**, it is used to determine next steps for the instructional path. By gathering and analyzing immediate assessment data, you can take facilitative actions to help students stay excited about and engaged in learning by providing just-in-time feedback and guidance to help them advance in their learning. The assessment–facilitation connection contributes to both the **atmosphere of continual motivation** and the **landscape of opportunities for academically rigorous learning**. As you explore facilitation strategies, keep assessment at the forefront of your mind; assessment should drive your facilitative actions.

Formative v. Summative Assessment

Assessments fall into two categories: formative and summative. Formative assessment refers to ongoing data-gathering that allows you to determine and address students' needs. Teachers use formative assessment to modify lessons and assignments. Summative assessment, on the other hand, is administered at the end of a unit or at a breakpoint (such as at the end of a semester, trimester, or school year) to see how well students have mastered the content. The value of summative assessment is that it can help determine necessary changes in instruction for future students and can inform the next teachers who will be working with the student.

You may have heard the statement, widely attributed to Douglas B. Reeves, that formative assessment is to a physical as summative assessment is to an autopsy. What a great analogy!

Formative assessments are used to assess student progress while they are in the midst of a unit of study. They allow you to make some in-the-moment decisions for instruction. If some students are showing great progress, you can offer some greater challenges; if some are having difficulty grasping the skill, you can record another video or add some *Learning Activities* to the *Activity List*. It's much the same as getting a physical while you're alive. Based on the data, you might change your diet, exercise more, take vitamins, etc. Formative assessments allow you to ensure that you're meeting the needs of all learners. Formative assessment is an important part of the **Hybrid Learning Environment**, contributing to the **structure of meaningful, data-driven learning**. Students can engage in formative assessment and share their results, thoughts, and plans with you; you can use formative assessment on a continual basis with students, wherever they are learning.

Summative assessments are given at the end of a unit of study or school year; standardized tests fall into this category as well. By the time students engage in the summative assessment, learning opportunities for that unit or year are over—thus, summative assessment is more like an autopsy. An autopsy occurs after a person dies, with the intent of shedding light on why they died. The information can be useful to others in the future, but it doesn't do anything for the person who died. Use summative assessment data to rethink your approach to instruction. That may include introducing topics in a more meaningful order, making better real-world connections to content, providing more and varied instructional activities, and so forth.

Both formative and summative assessment play a significant role in education. You use formative assessments to gauge student progress and make instructional decisions to further their learning. You use summative assessments to see how successful your instructional plan for a unit or portion of a year was. Essentially, formative assessment helps your students succeed; summative assessment helps you become a better educator.

Four Types of Formative Assessments

As you engage with your remote or in-class learners to monitor their progress, consider four types of formative assessments and ensure that you have a balance of them in your **Hybrid Learning Environment**:

- *Temperature Gauges*—These are short, in-the-moment assessments used to determine if the flow of information or action is appropriate. During a *Small-Group Mini-Lesson*, for instance, ask students to offer a thumbs-up, thumbs-down, or thumbs-middle in response to the question "Am I explaining this in a way that is working for you?" Note that if you ask students if they understand the content, they may be embarrassed to report that they do not; the question was phrased to evaluate *them*. When you ask them instead to evaluate the lesson, you will most likely obtain a more accurate assessment of their understanding, since the question asks them to evaluate *you*. When working remotely with students through videoconferencing, use polls to get a sense of how the lesson is progressing. In both remote and in-person situations, you can use an adjective check-in to have students share one adjective that shows how they are feeling about the content. The *Temperature Gauge Assessment* allows you to decide whether to continue on your planned path or modify your approach. If many students are stuck, you may want to linger on the topic and explain in alternate ways. If many students feel confident that they understand the content, you may want to cut short any continued discussion of the topic and move to an *Application Activity*. If some students are reporting that they do not understand the content, you may want to cut short the group engagement and offer varied opportunities for continuing. For example, some students can move on to related, independent activities while others may choose to remain with you. *Temperature Gauges* offer you a quick assessment of a moment in time, which often tells more about the effectiveness of the activity than overall content understanding.
- *Breakpoint Assessments*—These are more oriented toward assessing student understanding of the content, offered as students break from

one activity to move on to another. These include exit cards that ask the student to answer a question or write a response as they exit the class or lesson; one-sentence summaries to sum up learning after a video, lesson, or other instructional activity; quizzes; and the like. On a higher-order, application level, your students' *Efficacy Notebook* is, in essence, a collection of *Breakpoint Assessments* because students stop and answer questions after each activity. While the data from *Temperature Gauge Assessments* allow you to pivot in the midst of an activity, the data from *Breakpoint Assessments* allow you to plan for next steps for your students.

◆ *Student-Directed Assessments*—These fall under the *Assessment Activities* category of instructional activities described in Chapter 3. Students weigh in on their own progress and share it with you. These assessments might take the form of checklists, rubrics, and peer evaluations the student obtains and then shares with you with a response. They are also an aspect of the *Efficacy Notebook* in that students reflect on their own progress and report to you. *Student-Directed Assessments* offer you insights into how students perceive their progress, which may or may not match up with your own assessment. Any discrepancies warrant further discussion and assessment to determine the students' actual progress. Encourage students, too, to engage with their parents/caregivers to have them weigh in on the students' progress. Provide students with questions they can ask their parents/caregivers to obtain their perception of the students' progress. This is particularly useful when you find ways to engage parents/caregivers in the learning process. For example, if students are learning about the three branches of government, include instructional activities that have them sharing information, a drawing or infographic, or a description with their parents/caregivers to see if they think it's a good explanation. Later in the unit, you might offer scenarios they can discuss with their parents/caregivers to share ideas. In this way, parents/caregivers will be able to see how well they believe the student is progressing. Note: you should not assume the parents/caregivers have enough knowledge of the content to teach or assess it. Instead, you must carefully craft the interaction so as not to put more work on parents/caregivers and not to put the student in the position of receiving incorrect content information.

◆ *Comprehensive Assessments*—These tend to require more time than other assessments and focus on students demonstrating understanding of and the ability to apply content. This might include a performance-based assessment you review using a rubric, a portfolio, a test, and the like. Unlike *Breakpoint Assessments* that monitor student understanding of a narrow area of content, *Comprehensive Assessments* typically monitor student understanding of a broader area of content. For example, when addressing author's craft in writing, you might offer a *Breakpoint Assessment* in the form of an exit card on the use of a flashback: "Explain the author's use of a flashback, giving a definition, example, and the impact of that technique in the excerpt we read today." At a later point, you might offer a *Comprehensive Assessment* in the form of an essay critiquing the author's craft, asking the student to reference a variety of narrative elements and literary devices.

To continue with that last example of an author's craft, you would use *Temperature Gauges* to determine how effective the activity or lesson is in conveying the content. You would use *Breakpoint Assessments* to monitor student progress as the unit unfolds. *Student-Directed Assessments* would allow you to match your perception of the students' progress with theirs. *Comprehensive Assessments* would offer you a broader picture of student understanding and allow you to push their thinking to higher levels or offer alternative activities to solidify the learning. All these formative assessments provide you with valuable data to use when planning instruction.

STOP! Turn to Your *Efficacy Notebook*

Think about a recent or typical school week, and list the various ways in which you assessed student progress during the unity of study. Then, answer these questions.

1 How do your current assessments represent the four types of formative assessments, and how might you modify your approach to assessment as a result of this section?
2 What are some examples of ways in which you've used formative-assessment data to modify your instructional plan?
3 Which of the four types of formative assessment would be your "next frontier" for your professional growth?

The Facilitation Roadmap in a Hybrid Learning Environment

Attitude and mindset play an important role in learning. Interest, need, belief, confidence, persistence, resourcefulness, and resilience are just some of the attributes of a successful learner. While it is important to assess students' progress in a skill or concept, as discussed in the last section, it is equally important to assess and take action based on a student's mindset.

The "Facilitation Roadmap," reprinted from *Students Taking Charge* (Sulla, 2019a, p. 156, 2019b, p. 140), offers a guide for taking action based on the state of mind of the student (see Figure 7.1). This level of facilitation can take place whether students are in the classroom or at home.

You first observe the student to determine the student's mindset in tackling the content. Then, you take action based on what you observe. Notice that you are not assessing the student's understanding of the content; rather,

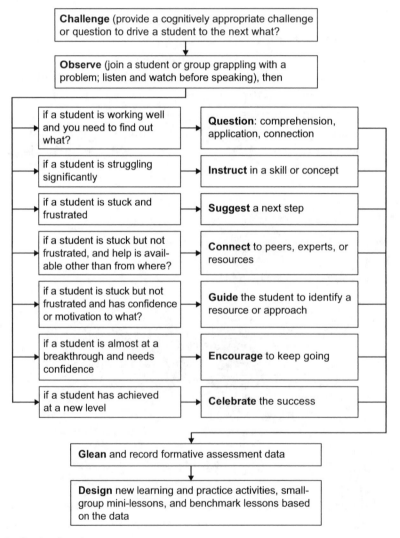

Figure 7.1 Facilitation Roadmap

you are attempting to determine if the current instructional activity is effective for the student.

If the student appears to be working well, you ask more questions to begin to assess student understanding of the content based on the activity. I once watched a student happily working through a stack of worksheets. Was he frustrated? No. Stuck? No. Bored? No. There was no need to intervene based on mindset; so, I began asking questions about the content to determine whether he was learning—and I determined that the answer was no! He was more focused on amassing a collection of worksheets so he could report on how much he accomplished rather than focusing on learning. If I were the teacher in this situation, I would have changed the instructional approach to focus less on completion and quantity and more on application and quality. Just because a student appears to be working well doesn't mean the situation doesn't warrant some additional questions to determine the effectiveness of the activity.

When students struggle significantly, they begin to lose confidence, their belief that they can learn, and interest. This is a dangerous situation. Any student who is on the edge of giving up deserves immediate assistance, typically in the form of direct instruction. Don't allow students to struggle to the point of giving up. Clearly, based on executive function development, some students may want to give up sooner than others, but that doesn't matter. If a student is at a breaking point, teach them, help them, provide the answers; then, provide a pathway to a next step that might be more attainable.

If a student is stuck and frustrated, but not at the breaking point, suggest a next step to move them in the right direction. For example, if a student is working to solve a word problem and understands the general approach to solving it but is not succeeding in setting up the math problem, suggest how they might set it up. Shifting back to the prior category, if the student is at the point of giving up, model how you would solve the problem and complete it for them. Then, offer another problem for the two of you to solve together. If the student is merely stuck, having you suggest a next step might be enough to fuel their continued progress.

If a student is stuck but not frustrated, and there are other resources available, point them to one or more resources: "How about looking in the *Resource Area* to see if there is a *How-To Sheet* for setting up a lab report?" (You know there is!) Point the student to activities on the *Activity List*, *Peer Experts*, or other resources. Help the student conduct a web search for assistance. If the student's mindset is still positive, helping them work through the challenge is a better approach than answering the question for them. You'll be building resilience! Sometimes, the goal of learning is not always simply about finding the answer.

If a student is stuck but seems to be confident they will figure it out, rather than pointing them to a resource, ask questions to help them see where they can find help: "Not sure how to conjugate that verb? Where do you think you could find help in conjugating this particular type of verb?" Let the student pause and consider that the answer might be in a textbook, on the web, in the *Resource Area*, and so forth. In this case, you'll be building resourcefulness!

If a student is working through a problem situation, generating possible solutions, and identifying resources, and seems to have the confidence that they will prevail, don't ruin the moment by injecting advice. Just build their confidence: "It looks like you're almost there; keep going!" "I love the way you are attacking the problem and locating resources; nice work!" Obviously, if you misread the situation, the student might respond in a way that lets you know they're more stuck than you thought. You can then decide on the appropriate action.

What about the student who succeeds in a learning challenge? Take a moment to stop and celebrate. Offer specific feedback on their mindset, resilience, resourcefulness, and overall approach. Ask them to share what was most difficult and/or what made them proudest. You can certainly ask them what they'll tackle next, or you can provide the next challenge. But take time to celebrate first.

As you use this approach, point out your decisions for action to the student. Teach students to assess their own mindset and advocate for help or celebrate success for themselves. You can also involve parents/caregivers in this process by asking them to assess their child's academic mindset, perhaps with some questions or definitions to help them better understand the categories. Let parents/caregivers share with you how your remote learners are succeeding in working on their own. You may want to share a modified version of the Facilitation Roadmap with them to encourage them to reach out to you if a student is stuck and ready to give up and to ask them to refrain from helping a student when it would be better to build resilience or resourcefulness. Becoming partners in the successful education of a student begins with sharing your approach with parents.

As you can see, assessment and facilitation go hand in hand. You assess students' content progress using the four types of formative assessment to modify the instructional plan to ensure learning. You assess students' mindsets as learners to help them build critical skills for lifelong learning, which will also lead to learning in the moment. Formative assessment and facilitation should be inextricably linked in your **Hybrid Learning Environment**.

I remember . . . my first day of tenth-grade English when my teacher distributed an anthology of literature that we would be reading and a grammar book. She told us to keep the grammar book at home and refer to it for our writing. She said that she would not teach grammar lessons as a rule, but rather review our writing and offer lessons and advice based on what she saw in our writing. And that she did. I remember receiving back my first paper with a big red D on it and marks all over the pages. I was stunned. After class, I met with her to ask how I received a D; I had always been an A student! She began by saying, well, first of all, the entire essay is written as one paragraph. I responded, "What's a paragraph?" I had been such a creative writer, my teachers did not apparently hold me to the conventions of structure and grammar. She pointed out some pages in that grammar book to which I should refer and offered me the opportunity to rewrite it. That I did, and I received a B, but that wasn't good enough for me. My next paper was better, but not an A. She, again, offered me some advice and referred me to some sections of that grammar book. I handed in a revision and received an A. My writing continued to improve, with my teacher facilitating my success. She never gave up on me; she just kept "recalculating" and offering me a path to success. When I successfully defended my doctoral dissertation in 1996, I drove to the school, picking up a bouquet of flowers along the way, and delivered my thanks and a copy of my dissertation, in which I acknowledged her for teaching me how to write. Thanks again, Phyllis Maloy—look at me now!

STOP! Turn to Your *Efficacy Notebook*

As you develop your **Hybrid Learning Environment** to include a **structure of meaningful, data-driven learning** and a **network of purposeful and productive facilitation of learning,** consider your current structures and strategies, and write about those you want to add to your repertoire. Then, answer these questions.

1   How will you use the Facilitation Roadmap in your own facilitation and with any co-teachers who may engage with you and your students?
2   How will you engage parents/caregivers as part of your network?
3   How can you make the assessment–facilitation partnership even more tightly aligned?

Administering Assessments in a Hybrid Learning Environment

Whole-class assessment can be very difficult in a **Hybrid Learning Environment**, as you cannot easily control the testing situation for students who are at home. Educational software and testing companies are attempting to develop online tests that reduce the possibility of students gaining answers elsewhere, so you might have options available to you. Generally, I recommend small-group assessment over whole-class assessment.

Small-Group Assessment

In a **Hybrid Learning Environment** where students are physically in a school building, teachers can offer most summative assessments and many formative assessments (such as quizzes, essays, exit cards, etc.) when students are physically in the classroom. The only need will be, perhaps, to have two versions of the assessment to ensure that the next day's group is not gaining an advantage by seeing the questions in advance from friends. In the case of fully remote instruction, teachers can use small-group assessment to gain more control over the assessment situation. Here are some options:

◆ Develop a performance-based assessment that requires the student to apply the learning to a new situation. This should be a situation that is not easily searched online. For example, after having taught the mathematical concept of scale, ask students to design the plan for a 3D virtual classroom space, drawn to scale, including the area of each section of the room, and the total perimeter and area, giving furniture options with dimensions supplied. Have a group of students on camera. Allow them to use their notes, but ask them to place cell phones away from them and indicate to their family members that they are taking a test. While the teacher cannot see everything, they can see students on video and potentially access any documents students are creating in the cloud to see how they are progressing. In the case of the previous example, where students are working on paper, I might ask students to point their camera on their paper so I can see them constructing their classrooms.

◆ Meet with a group of students through videoconference for a discussion, perhaps of a book they're reading. Ask questions, including directly to individuals, to have students explain or defend their opinions or claims, and listen to/capture evidence of content understanding for each participant. You might create an observational checklist to include, for example, defines key terms; uses key terms correctly in discussion; relates concepts to other concepts; demonstrates understanding; etc. Note: in the case of this performance-based task, each student's design will be different, so the possibility of finding answers on the web or from friends is eliminated. If, for any question, you have concerns about the situation—for example, if a student doesn't draw anything for a while and then suddenly constructs the entire classroom—follow up with specific questions to ensure that a student can answer appropriately and demonstrate understanding of the content. While some teachers may be concerned about cheating on assessments, when students are fully engaged in a **Hybrid Learning Environment**, they are more interested in solving real-world problems and learning what they need to know to accomplish that than in simply getting a good grade on an assessment: that's the goal!

◆ Offer a timed, online quiz, with a group of students on camera. Create a document and have students copy, rename, and share it with you, allowing you to move between the students' documents while they work. You see students on camera with microphones on; you also see their documents as they are answering.

One-on-One Assessment

At times, it is important to meet with just one student to assess progress. This might be necessary because of the teacher's uncertainty of a student's progress toward a particular standard, the level of differentiation in the classroom, or the nature of the content itself. For example, speech teachers and world language teachers need to hear an individual student speak. This may not always be possible during small-group assessment, thus requiring a one-on-one in-person or videoconference meeting.

The challenge of one-on-one assessment is that it removes the teacher from the rest of the class. In a **Hybrid Learning Environment**, where so much of the work toward mastery is occurring independently of teachers' live lessons, it is important for the teacher to be moving among the various learners, so any one-on-one assessments should be interlaced with facilitation time for the rest of the class. If a teacher meets with each individual student in succession, even for a few minutes, a full 40 minutes or more can pass during which the teacher is unavailable to the rest of the class.

For those situations where one-on-one assessment is preferable, keep the session to no more than 5 minutes. Keep the purpose focused, guided by a digital or paper grid for collecting the assessment data. Keep the student focused on the assessment topic. Students may use this time to discuss other issues; decide if those issues can be addressed elsewhere, such as through a *Small-Group Mini-Lesson* or discussion. Manage your time to conduct one-on-one assessment sessions interlaced with *Small-Group Mini-Lessons, Benchmark Discussions*, and other small-group engagement so you're not unavailable to any student for long periods of time.

Equity Matters

Given that equity is about ensuring that *all* students have the tools, resources, opportunities, and access they need to succeed in a culturally responsive and nonthreatening environment, the facilitation–assessment pair becomes even more important. Regularly assess whether students have the tools and resources they each need. Regularly assess whether you've curated a learning environment with ample opportunities and access for all. Regularly assess your learning environment to ensure that it is culturally responsive and non-threatening to all learners. This **structure of meaningful, data-driven learning** will make it easy to build your **network of purposeful and productive facilitation of learning**.

The Big Three: Learning, SEL, Efficacy

When you think of your role as similar to that of a GPS, continually assessing the situation and taking action based on that information, you can easily address the goals of student learning and SEL, and, ultimately, efficacy. Most people think of assessment as an after-the-fact moment in time; however, when you consider how it can be paired with facilitation to drive your instructional curation decisions, you'll produce better results in student learning. When you also hold dear the goal of building SEL in students, you create "observable" criteria that you can assess and address through facilitation. Through personalized facilitation to support students in achieving their goals, experiencing successes, and building confidence, you build student efficacy.

STOP! Turn to Your *Efficacy Notebook*

Consider the need for assessment in your **Hybrid Learning Environment**, and answer these questions.

1   What assessment strategies are you currently using that are working?

> 2   As you think of an upcoming unit of study or unit you are design-
>   ing for the future, what plans can you develop for both formative
>   and summative assessment?
> 3   After reading this chapter, what are your ideas for melding assess-
>   ment and facilitation in your **Hybrid Learning Environment**?

References

Sulla, N. (2015). *It's not what you teach but how: 7 insights for making the CCSS work for you.* New York: Routledge.

Sulla, N. (2019a). *Students taking charge in grades K–5: Inside the learner-active, technology-infused classroom.* New York: Routledge.

Sulla, N. (2019b). *Students taking charge in grades 6–12: Inside the learner-active, technology-infused classroom.* New York: Routledge.

8

In Pursuit of Equity

Equity—it's not about opportunity alone; it's about opportunity and access.

 Imagine!

Achieving an equitable learning environment translates to providing all students with an unobstructed pathway to success. Imagine classrooms of socioeconomically and culturally diverse students with a wide range of backgrounds, experiences, and abilities all succeeding at high levels! They own their learning; they make decisions about how, when, and with whom they will learn. Some students gravitate more toward collaborating, while others prefer individual work; some are auditory learners, while some are visual learners, but all have access to the resources they need to learn. Students report feeling good about themselves and their chances for success in school. They report feeling that their in-school and at-home learning experiences make them feel like they are part of a supportive and safe community. Teachers engage with students to help them make good choices for their learning and become more aware of themselves as individuals in a collective community of learners. Teachers "see" students from academic, social, emotional, and cultural perspectives, and design learning environments that meet the needs of all students. Students view teachers as resources and invaluable guides in their pursuit of learning.

Rebooting Our Thinking

Students under the age of 25, even with typical brain development, most likely do not have fully developed executive function that would enable them to make appropriate decisions, take actions with a clear understanding of future consequences, and apply significant levels of higher-order reasoning. That pretty much sums up your K–12 population. This is an important reality introduced in Chapter 6 and discussed in more detail in the book *Building Executive Function: The Missing Link to Student Achievement* (Sulla, 2018). Therefore, we need to dispel the belief that if students don't show up for the lesson, put in the effort, or pay attention, and they don't learn, it's just their fault. One of the goals of school is to build in students the skills they need to learn, rather than assuming that they already have them.

All the teachers I've known *want* all of their students to learn; the challenge is always *how*. It comes down to a shift in thinking from equal to equitable. When you offer a lesson to all students at a certain time, that's equal. When you offer the same lesson or assignment to all, that's equal. There is a misconception that "equal" is synonymous with "fair." In a learning environment, where the goal is to ensure that *all* students learn at high levels, providing each student with personalized learning should be a given. That sort of personalization is common practice in other fields, such as health care. Medical staff focused on addressing different patients' needs differentiate their treatment to meet individual needs; equal is not fair. In the same way, educators need to focus on addressing different learners' needs and differentiating their instructional approach; when it comes to a learning environment, equal is not fair. Fair means offering *all* students what they need to have opportunity and access to high-quality instruction and related learning experiences.

Therefore, that lesson at that specific time, and that particular assignment, may not be what a particular student needs; so equal does not necessarily produce learning. Equity means providing learners with the resources and support *they* need to succeed. Teachers who embrace equity in instruction use ongoing formative assessment to inform their instructional decisions, apply a lens of cultural awareness, differentiate instruction to meet individual students' needs, and create a classroom environment that allows all students to feel physically and emotionally safe while having some control over their own learning.

Though some students thrive in remote and **Hybrid Learning Environments**, working remotely can present even greater challenges to students than learning in the physical classroom, and the achievement gap can widen. Taking an equity approach to designing your **Hybrid Learning Environment** is more important than ever. It's time to reboot our thinking from equal opportunity to equitable opportunity!

Seven Lenses of Instructional Equity

Figure 8.1 offers you seven lenses through which to assess and design your **Hybrid Learning Environment**. Each of these lenses should be evident in all aspects of your reinvented classroom experience for your students:

- ◆ Opportunity
- ◆ Access
- ◆ Representation
- ◆ Empowerment
- ◆ Relationships
- ◆ Authenticity
- ◆ Cultural Responsiveness

Opportunity and Access

Equity—it's not about opportunity alone; it's about opportunity *and* access. If you teach, students have the opportunity to learn. If a student doesn't understand what you're saying because of a lack of prerequisite knowledge or language differences, they have no access to that opportunity to learn. If you provide *Learning Activities*, students have the opportunity to learn. If those activities are heavily text-based and a student's cultural background is one of oral traditions, thus making verbal information easier to comprehend, that student may lack access to that opportunity.

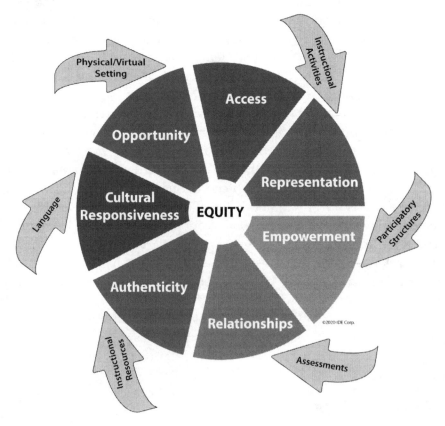

Figure 8.1 IDE Corp.'s Seven Lenses of Equity

Add to these descriptions the challenges of the 2020 pandemic and situations where students are learning from home. What if a student lives in a home where siblings have to share a computing device? When you offer a 10:00 a.m. lesson as an opportunity to learn, if that student cannot use the computing device at that time, they miss access to that opportunity. Sometimes, older students have to take care of their younger siblings because their parent(s) or caregiver(s) have to go to work. Those caregiving students may not have access to lessons at the time you are offering them. Some older students have to go to work to contribute to the family's income; they may not be able to engage in learning opportunities at the same time they are offered. An equitable instructional plan includes ensuring time alignment such that all opportunities to learn are accessible to *all* students, even when their time needs differ from those of others.

The list could go on, but the point is, as you design your **landscape of opportunities for academically rigorous learning**, remember that when it comes to equity—it's not about opportunity alone; it's about opportunity and access. Given your students' home situations, cultural backgrounds, cognitive levels, and other characteristics affecting learning, are you providing access for all?

All students in your classroom can learn at high levels. That's not a buzz phrase; it's a reality that requires the opportunity–access connection. No matter how great the opportunity to learn, if students cannot *access* that opportunity, they will fall short of learning goals—and it will not be their fault. Ensuring that opportunities are coupled with access builds the **landscape of opportunities for academically rigorous learning** in your **Hybrid Learning Environment**.

As you reinvent the classroom experience, you'll gain some unexpected benefits. For example, once you provide access for all through greater dependence on video and independent "learn anywhere, anytime" *Learning Activities*, students who are absent from school due to illness will no longer have to miss out on learning opportunities. When they are feeling well enough, they can access videos and follow their *Activity List*, which provides them with both opportunity and access.

STOP! Turn to Your *Efficacy Notebook*

Think about your classroom or school, the difference between the opportunities you create for learning, and the level of access students have. That access includes technology, time alignment, and use of varied types of instructional activities. Then, answer these questions.

1   In what ways do all your students (every single one of them) have access to learning anywhere, anytime?

> 2   What are a few more steps you can take in this direction immediately to strengthen the opportunity–access connection?
> 3   What are some bigger steps that may take you more time that will provide your students with an even more equitable learning environment than you have now?

The remaining five lenses of equity all stem from the opportunity–access connection.

Representation

During the 2020 Emmy Awards, actress Cynthia Erivo said, "When we don't see ourselves on television, we start to feel invisible. When we do see ourselves, it reminds us that we are invincible." Representation matters! It shapes the future of every one of your students.

Have you heard of Marley Dias, the then 11-year-old who, tired of reading about white boys and their dogs in her school books, launched the #1000BlackGirlBooks campaign and ended up collecting more than ten times that many books? Her own book, *Marley Dias Gets It Done: And So Can You* (2018), begins with "If only" statements:

> If only there'd been one book at school . . . just one . . . about a black girl and her dog. . . .
> A brainiac black girl astronaut with her trailblazing space poodle, exploring the rings of Saturn. . . .
> A fierce black girl fashion designer with her frisky Rottweiler on a rhinestone leash, owning the streets of the city. . . .
> A fearless black girl forensic archaeologist, with her inquisitive collie uncovering the fossil remains of some prehistoric species. . . .
>
> (pp. 18–19)

Representation matters! Students need to see others who look like them and who have accomplished great things. Students learn from role models; they aspire to new heights because of their role models. In reading literature, readers put themselves in the place of the character and learn to make life choices. Shouldn't those characters represent the reader some of the time?

What does your physical and/or virtual classroom look like? What images do students see on the walls, including the virtual walls of your virtual classroom? Do they reflect the cultures of your students? Do they offer all students a vision for their future through the faces of the heroes and accomplished professionals who are displayed?

In your *Priming Plan* (Chapter 2), what famous personalities are students encountering in their studies? How representative are they of your students? Do all students have access to images and stories of people who look like them who have gone on to excel in the areas of business, journalism, math, science, the arts, technology, politics, sports, entrepreneurship, and more? Watch for representational bias, as I stated earlier! Do your black students only see images of sports and music figures while your white students see images of scientists and politicians? Do your girls see themselves amidst those who excel in science and math? (Shout-out to Olay for their float in the 2020 Macy's Thanksgiving Day parade that depicted a woman of color as an astronaut, surrounded by STEM materials; they are committed to increasing the number of women and multicultural women in STEM careers.) Be mindful of the stories your representational patterns are showing. While classrooms are opportunities to learn, those that provide representation for the learners also provide them with access to that learning, allowing them to see themselves as successful. This is an important part of how you design your physical and virtual classroom.

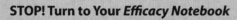

STOP! Turn to Your *Efficacy Notebook*

Write about the **culture of social and emotional learning** that exists in your classroom through the self-awareness opportunities your students have to "see themselves."

1   What more could you do to ensure representation in your classroom decorations?
2   What more could you do to ensure representation in the videos and websites you select or design as learning activities?
3   What more could you do to ensure representation in the project- and problem-based tasks you use?

Empowerment

A common goal today is to increase student engagement. Engagement occurs often when you have a strong opportunity–access connection paired with a compelling reason to learn (Chapter 4). However, just beyond engagement lies empowerment—being given some control over and responsibility for the student's own learning. Provide students with a level of autonomy by having them make some decisions about each of the following:

◆ How they learn—selecting appropriate and interesting instructional activities from a differentiated *Activity List*. Your role is to curate that *Activity List* and provide guidance for all students in how to make the right choices for their learning.

◆ When they learn—scheduling when they will engage in the activities from the *Activity List*. While you're teaching "live," *Benchmark Discussions* and some other forms of synchronous engagement (Chapter 5) will occur at specific times, and preferably with choices so all students have access to these opportunities. Students should then be empowered to plan the remaining time for their day and week. You may have specific activities that need to be completed by certain times; that's fine to indicate on the *Activity List*. Students should be able to schedule those and still have significant choice about when they learn.

◆ With whom they'll learn—selecting opportunities to work independently, in pairs, or in groups. While you may designate some activities to be completed independently, in pairs, or in small groups, students should still be empowered to have some choice as to if and when they prefer to learn with others.

◆ What they learn—deciding on skills and concepts they want to learn. While your curriculum will have very specific concepts and skills to address, there can always be room for students to pursue related interests, especially if you are using a PBL approach to instruction (Chapter 4). A middle school science teacher launched a unit on designing an ecosystem to support life on Mars, given that scientists had now determined that water exists there. One of her students was equally fascinated by Triton, one of Neptune's moons that is also believed to have water just beneath the surface. He asked if he could design a biodome to support life on Triton; his teacher said yes. That's what empowerment looks like.

◆ Why they learn—identifying real-world problems to solve that relate to the curriculum. If a student raises concerns about the level of pollution in a local lake, consider using that as the anchor for learning the curricular content, if you can create a fit. While, again, you most likely have a set curriculum in place, you increase empowerment when you allow students to identify the problems and challenges they want to tackle.

The road to efficacy begins with engagement and empowerment. Designing a **Hybrid Learning Environment** that empowers students will position them to make a difference in the world outside and beyond school.

STOP! Turn to Your *Efficacy Notebook*

Your **foundation for student responsibility for learning** begins by empowering students to take responsibility! Consider the ways in which you empower your students, and then answer these questions.

1   What choices and areas of empowerment do students already have in your **Hybrid Learning Environment**?
2   How can you provide students with greater empowerment in the areas of how, when, and with whom they learn?
3   How can you provide students with greater empowerment in the areas of what and why they learn?

Relationships

Human beings are drawn to relationships with others and enjoy "belonging." Meaningful adult relationships play a key role in student learning (Cookson, 2017). When you feel a sense of safety and build positive relationships with others, you are more likely to allow those people to influence you enough to learn from them.

Your brain has two "gatekeepers" for allowing information to move through the brain to the sections that address learning. The reticular activating system (RAS) of the brain continually scans the environment for threats or rewards. If the brain senses a threat, it shifts to "fight or flight" mode and does not process the information in learning mode. Threats can come in the form of microaggressions, bullying, explicit or implicit bias against the student, teachers' dislike for the student, and more. When faced with such threats, the student can become defensive, which is not a situation conducive to learning.

Assuming there are no threats, the brain will move the information to the limbic brain. This part of the brain handles motivation, emotion, memory, and learning; it is connected to the prefrontal cortex, the area of the brain responsible for many executive function skills and for intellectuality. You can help your students' brains tend toward learning by ensuring that threats are eliminated, and by building relationships with your students so they feel emotionally safe.

This can be accomplished, in part, by asking yourself how you feel about each of your students. What beliefs do you hold about them? Are there any students you favor, and why? Are there any students you dislike, and why? Are there any students you feel won't be able to excel in your class, and why? Seek to uncover your own implicit biases. We all have them, even if we hope we don't; reflect, uncover, and shift your thinking.

Next, taking into account any situations you need to address from the last paragraph to ensure you believe in your students and their ability to succeed, get to know your students beyond the surface. What beliefs do they hold? What experiences frame their lives? What motivates them? How do they feel in your **Hybrid Learning Environment**? Spend synchronous time (both one on one and in small groups) connecting and building relationships with students.

STOP! Turn to Your *Efficacy Notebook*

Write about the **culture of social and emotional learning** that exists in your classroom through the relationships you build.

1 How do you build meaningful relationships with each of your students?
2 If your students took a survey, what are the top three adjectives they would use to describe you? Write about how those adjectives speak to building meaningful relationships.
3 How else might you get to know your students well, going beneath the surface?

Authenticity

All students deserve to have the best opportunities and access to learn; all students deserve to have their instructional activities be meaningful to them. To increase student engagement and the likelihood of long-term retention, learning should be authentic and relevant to students.

When providing a frame of reference and backdrop, be sure the examples and scenarios you use are authentic—they are realistic, culturally relevant, and meaningful to your students. If you are engaging in some problem solving or reading related to skiing, and you have a large number of students from South America, spend a little time discussing the sport, including places in South America where you can ski and why. Be mindful of your students and their life experiences as you set the stage for learning.

When using problem- and project-based learning (Chapter 4), develop and/or have your students develop tasks that relate to solving problems or tackling challenges that are authentic to your students. Students living in urban environments can investigate global heat; they can consider how to tackle prevalent social issues in countries of their heritage, including illiteracy, poverty, hunger, racism, gender equity, and more; they can tackle equity issues in their school or community. This doesn't mean every PBL task should be about the local community or directly related to the student, but students should be able to identify an authentic connection between themselves and the content.

As you can see, representation, cultural responsiveness, and authenticity work in concert with one another. Engage students in problem solving related to their own interests, backgrounds, and communities. Let them see themselves represented in the materials and purposes of the curricular units.

STOP! Turn to Your *Efficacy Notebook*

Consider your **Hybrid Learning Environment** and the tasks and assignments you ask your students to complete. Then, answer these questions.

1 What are some examples of authentic assignments and activities you offer your students?
2 How might you make your assignments and activities even more authentic?
3 What real-world problems exist that relate to both your curriculum and to your students?

Cultural Responsiveness

Zaretta Hammond (2015) speaks to the importance of moving beyond surface culture (holidays, rituals, food, etc.) and shallow culture (norms of engagement and communication) to deep culture: "the tacit knowledge and unconscious assumptions that govern our worldview" (p. 23). To that end, she presents two cultural archetypes for teachers to consider: collectivism and individualism, and text dependence and oral traditions.

Collectivism and Individualism

The United States and Western European countries tend to have a more individualistic culture, characterized by competition and valuing the efforts of the individual. Many countries in Africa, Asia, Central America, and South America tend to be more collectivist in nature, valuing the collaborative efforts of a group. When students from diverse cultures approach learning in school, their worldview tends toward collectivism or individualism; teaching them in ways that are opposite to their worldview may not produce the best results. Allowing students to learn in ways that make sense to them provides greater access to those learning opportunities. Then, creating a balance between their natural learning inclinations and that of the country in which they are currently living will position them for success in life and career as they learn to navigate their way in the world.

In a **Hybrid Learning Environment**, your *Activity List* (Chapter 3) provides students with a variety of ways in which to learn, from which they choose. Be mindful of the cultural differences of the students in your classroom and provide activities that are both individualistic and collaborative in nature. Know that while some *Learning Activities* may be completed in pairs or groups, all students are expected to demonstrate individual mastery so they are not dependent on another person to carry them through. In a collectivist society, the goal is interdependence: we all contribute to the learning process, yet we all learn and can stand on our own.

Text Dependence and Oral Traditions

While storytelling and oral traditions were the earliest form of communication, Western Europe and the United States developed as text-dependent societies. Heavy emphasis is placed on reading texts, with that being one of the first goals of public education. In some other countries, including African and South American nations, passing along information has relied more on oral traditions. That may be due in part to a society's inclination toward collectivism; it may be due in part to the ability of one's ancestors to read and write, thus leaning more toward oral traditions. Those two different cultural backgrounds position students to lean more toward visual preferences or auditory preferences for taking in information and for communicating. Cultural responsiveness requires being aware of these cultural differences and ensuring that opportunities for learning offer access for all. Offer your students opportunities to engage with content and with one another through text as well as verbal conversations.

STOP! Turn to Your *Efficacy Notebook*

As you think of ensuring cultural responsiveness in your **Hybrid Learning Environment**, answer these questions.

1 How will you foster opportunities for both collectivism and individualism through the following:

   a *Instructional Videos*
   b *Learning Activities*

> c   Problem- and project-based tasks
> d   *Benchmark Discussions*
>
> 2   How will you foster opportunities for both oral traditions and text-dependency through these:
>
> a   *Instructional Videos*
> b   *Learning Activities*
> c   Problem- and project-based tasks
> d   *Benchmark Discussions*

The Drivers of Your Equity Attainment

The seven lenses of equity represent the underlying areas and beliefs that must be present in the learning environment. They are reflected across six areas:

- *Physical and Virtual Setting*—your physical classroom and the virtual representations and Learning Management System sites you create
- *Instructional Activities*—your *Learning, Practice, Application, Assessment*, and *Reflection Activities*
- *Participatory Structures*—ways in which students participate with other students and the adults in their learning
- *Assessments*—both formative and summative
- *Instructional Resources*—texts, worksheets, videos, websites, and other materials used in the learning process
- *Language*—the words that your students hear and read from you

As you build your awareness of the seven lenses, keep looking for ways you can better attain equity in your **Hybrid Learning Environment**. Keep self-assessing; keep talking with students; keep honoring the voices of students; keep reflecting! Equity is essential to ensuring students learn at high levels; equity provides students with meaningful experiences through which to build SEL; equity eliminates the barriers to students building a strong sense of efficacy.

I remember . . . going to junior high school in the 1960s, toward the end of the civil rights movement in America. My school was 70% black and 30% white. I was painfully aware of the divide between the two groups; we were not melded into one learning community. What struck me most, however, was that there were no black students in my classes. Where were they? I remember thinking something wasn't right about this. I only saw the black students when changing classes, and in physical education class. Fast forward 50 years, the needle has moved; but not that much! While we have seen changes in schools, we still have far to go to overturn the biases and barriers that challenge equity. Thank you for reading this book and this chapter. Your efforts will move schools toward greater equity.

 STOP! Turn to Your *Efficacy Notebook*

As you think about how you are attaining equity for all your students in your **Hybrid Learning Environment**, answer these questions.

1 How are the seven lenses of equity reflected in each of the six instructional areas? It may be easiest to make a chart of the seven lenses down the side and six areas across the top. Then, fill in each cell.
2 What more can you do or what can you do differently to further advance equity in your **Hybrid Learning Environment**?

References

Cookson Jr., P. W. (2017). *Exploring equity issues: Building relationships for student success.* Washington, DC: American Institutes for Research.

Diaz, M. (2018). *Marley Dias gets it done and so can you.* New York: Scholastic.

Hammond, Z. (2015). *Culturally responsive teaching & the brain: Promoting authentic engagement and rigor among culturally and linguistically diverse students.* Thousand Oaks, CA: Corwin.

Sulla, N. (2018). *Building executive function: The missing link to student achievement.* New York: Routledge.

9

The Home Connection

In a powerful home–school connection, parents/caregivers are not home-schooling; they are managing a home-based learning environment.

 ## Imagine!

Imagine that when students are learning from home, they follow a routine of getting up, getting ready for school, planning lunch in advance, and logging into your Learning Management System at the same time every day, where possible. They have a work location that provides them with a lighted, quiet space to work, with resources they may need. Imagine that, as the teacher, you have developed a strong partnership with your students' parents/caregivers. You provide a comprehensive instructional program; they manage the home-based learning environment. Even though you have different perspectives on the learning process, you operate as one, united support system in the students' learning process. With everyone agreeing to take responsibility for different aspects of the learning environment, maintaining strong communication, and supporting one another's efforts, students win!

Home-Based Learning

When students are working to learn at home, either entirely or on a rotating basis with attending school, parents and caregivers become a more present member of the learning community than ever before. To establish a **network of purposeful and productive facilitation of learning**, you need to deliberately and purposefully include them in the design of your **Hybrid Learning Environment**. They can play an important role in managing a home-based learning environment to maximize student success. They will contribute to other attributes of a **Hybrid Learning Environment** as well; however, enlisting them in helping to facilitate student learning is important. That doesn't necessarily mean that you want them to engage with the content; you want them to facilitate learning by managing a home-based learning environment.

In a powerful home–school connection, parents/caregivers are not home-schooling; they are managing a home-based learning environment. It's important to assure parents/caregivers that you are taking responsibility for their child's education; you are designing the academic plan, whether students are in school or at home. As managers of a home-based learning environment, parents/caregivers are serving as a critical partner with you in facilitating student learning, fostering their child's SEL, and, ultimately, building student efficacy.

Start early, preferably before school starts each year, with an emphasis on the opening weeks of school, and engage parents/caregivers in partnering with you. Help them understand the eight elements of a home-based learning environment that will be described in this chapter. You might create a booklet, web page, or checklist; record a video; or have them watch my videos on home-based learning and access resources at https://4theparents.idecorp. com.

You needn't leave it all up to the parents/caregivers. Work with your students to establish your expectations for their home-based learning environment, holding them responsible for setting it up. That way, parents/caregivers are supporting the students in taking charge of their own learning.

A Pledge to the Children

Everyone enters a situation with their own perspective, and school is certainly no exception. The advent of remote/hybrid learning has raised some issues that may need to be addressed in your classroom. Parents/caregivers often have their ideas as to what teaching should look like; teachers have their ideas as to what they think parent support should look like. Sometimes, the two perspectives don't align. The more you work to build that alignment, the better experience your students will have as they enjoy learning anywhere, anytime.

Have you considered engaging parents/caregivers in creating a joint pledge to support the academic and social and emotional growth of the children? Think about what you will promise your parents/caregivers. Think about what you would like from them. Consider engaging them in writing a joint pledge, asking them what they would like from you as the teacher and what role they would be willing to play. Figure 9.1 offers an example of a Pledge to the Children.

You might start by sending home a survey to parents/caregivers and repeating that process during the year. It's always a good idea to state up

---

We, the teachers, parents, and caregivers pledge to take joint responsibility for the academic and social and emotional growth of _____. As a united force of support, we pledge:

Teachers
- To provide you with many ways to learn, so that you can learn in ways that make sense to you
- To check in with you daily, whether in person, through videoconference, or messaging,
- To be available in a timely manner to help you when you're stuck
- To get to know you so that I can better develop your learning path
- To support your parents / caregivers in their support of you

Parents and Caregivers
- To work with you to set up a home learning environment that will maximize your success
- To allow you to productively struggle in learning and not jump in too soon to fix things for you
- To ask you questions and listen as you share about what you are learning and how it will help you in your life
- To help you learn how to study, I will share strategies that worked for me and seek new ways that work for you
- To support your teachers in their support of you

Teacher(s):   Parents/Caregiver(s):

_____   _____

_____   _____

_____   _____

_____

_____

_____

Figure 9.1 A Pledge to the Children

front that the purpose of the survey is to help you gain insights from the parents'/caregivers' perspective so you can make decisions about the instructional program. Be sure to include that you hope they realize it is not possible to implement every idea but that the collection of feedback from across the class will help you tremendously in making this the best year possible for their child.

Then, send home a draft and ask parents/caregivers to join you in a partnership for the success of their children. You need to be careful, though. Remember that you are responsible for the education of your students. You are essentially asking parents/caregivers to be supportive and, in the case of students working from home, to manage a home-based learning environment. You do not want parents/caregivers to misconstrue this as an attempt to have them do your job. When parents/caregivers work together, better outcomes emerge for students. That requires clear and frequent communication, and demonstrated respect for parents/caregivers, teachers, and children. You can help to establish that partnership.

Create resources to help students and parents/caregivers succeed at managing a home-based learning environment based on the eight elements that follow. These resources might include direction sheets, videos, and checklists.

We know that parents/caregivers are an important part of a student's learning world. So, let's take a look at eight elements of a home-based learning environment that you can help your students' parents/caregivers establish and manage.

Eight Elements of a Home-Based Learning Environment

Visualize a student working from home to learn. What would position them to meet with the most success as they watch their teachers' videos, read texts, engage with a website, draw, and so forth? These eight elements represent the basics of setting up a home-based learning environment:

- ◆ Structure
- ◆ Projects
- ◆ Resources
- ◆ Downtime
- ◆ Conversation
- ◆ Balance
- ◆ Celebration Zone
- ◆ Reflection

Consider how these elements would help your students and create a plan to offer them, and other elements, to the parents/caregivers of your students to support their learning at home.

Structure

Human beings enjoy having some level of structure that provides normalcy and what I like to refer to as "the knowns." There are so many unknowns we all face in the course of a day, it's nice to be grounded in some level of structure—though some of us prefer less or more structure than others.

Time

Students should wake up and get ready for school at the same time every day. If you're teaching students who are alternating between home and the school building, it's important for them to connect online from home, or get started working if they lack internet access, at the same time every day. That time should be at least 30 minutes after waking up because the brain, upon waking, is in a state of sleep inertia and not quite ready to learn (Vallat, Meunier, Nicolas, & Ruby, 2018). It is difficult for the body to adjust to waking up at vastly different times every day, so creating a structure for waking, eating, and sleeping at consistent times will help students in their school endeavors.

Once they are "in school," students should manage their time across the day, preferably creating a schedule. Figures 9.2 and 9.3 offer examples of schedules that students can use to map out their day. Provide your parents/caregivers with a schedule students will use at home to plan their day and monitor their progress. It may be an online schedule they design as part of your Learning Management System, in which case you can record a video to explain how to access it and what you expect from students. It may be a paper or digital document they use; again, you can record an explanatory video. The more you inform your parents/caregivers of your expectations and the more structures you offer them to use at home, the better your **Hybrid Learning Environment** will run. Plus, having students set and follow a schedule contributes to the **foundation of student responsibility for learning**.

To position students for success in scheduling how they will use their time, consider the following:

◆ Up to 7 years old—Provide options and have students either move corresponding images into an ordered list or number them in their order of preference. Based on their level of executive function, the

Name: _____

Day: _____

Activity (Write or Cut and Paste)	I did it! I feel . . .
	🙂 😐 🙁
	🙂 😐 🙁
	🙂 😐 🙁
	🙂 😐 🙁
	🙂 😐 🙁

Figure 9.2 Sample Early Childhood Schedule

youngest learners may need to schedule the morning separately from the afternoon, rather than attempting to plan an entire day.

◆ Ages 7–10—Have students create a chronological schedule that includes start and end times for an entire day.

◆ Ages 10 and up—Have students create a chronological schedule that includes start and end times for an entire week.

Routine

Routines create a sense of normalcy; upon entering school, students carry out routines, such as storing their book bags or heading to their lockers, logging onto a classroom website, and so forth. Have the student develop a daily checklist for a morning routine and carry it out every day, whether they are learning in school or at home. This may include making the bed, brushing teeth, taking a shower, eating breakfast, and so forth.

In school, students generally eat lunch at the same time every day. Encourage students and parents/caregivers to replicate this schedule at home. At a designated time each day, students should head to the refrigerator to retrieve their lunch, which they or their parents/caregivers made in the morning.

Name: _____

Date: _____

Schedule your whole day at the start of a day or the day before. At the end of the day, reflect on how you did

Start Time	End Time	Activity	Done

Reflection:

Figure 9.3 Sample Student Schedule

Stopping to first figure out what to eat and then having to prepare it during the lunch hour will decrease the amount of downtime for the student and will increase stress.

Help students and parents/caregivers create a routine for the end of the school day. Keeping in mind that the purpose of homework is to have the practice spaced apart from the learning, explain to students that they should stop working after school, engage in other activities, and then set an appointed time for homework each night. After the school day, however, their routine might include putting away resources and straightening up their work area. The times for engaging in the before- and after-school routines can be added to the schedule described in the previous section or may be developed separately. Work with students to build a daily routine for before and after school and have them develop a video or document to explain it to their parents/caregivers.

Remote Learning Zone

In creating structure, students should establish a Remote Learning Zone at which to work when they are at home (okay, that's a fancy way of saying a work desk or table). It should be a location where students can easily work and be surrounded by resources they may need. It may be at the kitchen table or counter or at a desk, but the day should not begin with trying to find a spot in which to work. The Remote Learning Zone should have a hard surface for writing and a setup where the computer is in a comfortable spot. Attempting to engage in schoolwork by lying on the floor or from the couch without a desktop surface is probably not the best choice.

The key here is to provide students with a good deal of structure to support learning at home. Consistency and an easy approach to daily work will allow students to focus on what matters: your lessons, activities, assignments, and time with them. Provide parents/caregivers with checklists, videos, descriptions, and anything else you think will help them understand the importance of structure in a home-based learning environment.

STOP! Turn to Your *Efficacy Notebook*
Think of how you can help parents/caregivers create structure in the home-based learning environment to support student learning.

1   What sort of structure do you want in place for your students at home?

> 2   What tools can you create for parents/caregivers to help them set up structure at home?
> 3   How can you involve your students in designing a resource for parents/caregivers related to managing a home-based learning environment?

Projects

Projects energize and engage students; they help create connections to improve learning and retention. You've already explored the power of problem-, project-, place-, profession-, and pursuit-based learning in Chapter 4. Extend this level of engagement and **atmosphere of continual motivation** to the home-based learning environment as well as through a project in which students can engage with their parents/caregivers. It may be a pursuit-based problem that students will tackle and discuss with their parents/caregivers, or it could be a joint project to engage parents/caregivers with the student.

Partner with parents/caregivers to determine projects in which students could engage in their homes. Maybe it's organizing the cabinets, painting a mural on the wall, developing some sort of collection, solving a real-world problem of interest, engaging in a charitable project, solving a local challenge or problem, and so forth.

As students engage in at-home projects, they should consider how what they are learning through school applies to their project. Have them make connections between everything you're teaching and their at-home projects. Help parents/caregivers engage in conversation around the projects on which students are working. Create a student–parent/caregiver partnership for completing a project. Students will bring their learning to the table in tackling the project, and they will gain so much by collaborating with a parent or caregiver. Give parents/caregivers a role in developing a project in the home-based learning environment. This collaboration will enrich your **landscape of opportunities for academically rigorous learning**.

I remember . . . when I was in sixth grade learning American history and I was tasked with developing a project of my choice connected to the unit of study. I shared my assignment with my parents; Dad thought it would be great to carve a bust of the President out of plaster of Paris. I went along with the idea. I remember him turning over the greased bucket and watching the hardened plaster slide out. I then said, "So now what do we do?" To this day, it's one of those funny moments I will never forget. He looked at me and said, "Well, now we just carve away anything that doesn't look like the President!" We then raided my mom's kitchen drawers to find carving utensils. I had a great time working on this with my dad, though I must admit, he carved away a lot more of what didn't look like the President than I did. When I brought the bust into school, I just looked at my teacher; she and I both understood what had happened: parents gone wild! (Dad then carved a bust of Shakespeare, as he was having so much fun.) It felt great to work on this joint project. I'm sure with some parameters, and perhaps a rubric and some norms, teachers could engage students with others in their homes to collaborate on a project. Depending on the situation, that may include significant collaboration or having parents/caregivers offer feedback, answer interview questions, or share and discuss ideas with the student. I know my time working on school projects with my dad was priceless. RIP, Dad!

Design Process

When students are tackling a problem or challenge, using a design process helps organize their thoughts and actions toward success. Consider sharing a design process with parents/caregivers so that they can help students follow a methodical process for problem solving at home. IDE Corp.'s design process (see Figure 9.4) includes the following steps:

1 Formulate—Define the problem or challenge.
2 Explore—Research the problem or challenge; generate questions and pursue answers.
3 Ideate—Freely brainstorm many possible solutions.
4 Sift—Consider each solution in terms of feasibility and effectiveness.
5 Simulate—Create a prototype solution to test.
6 Advocate—Share the solution with a meaningful audience.

Figure 9.4 IDE Corp.'s Design Process

Our YouTube channel (youtube.com/c/IDECorp/videos) includes videos on the design process that could be shared with parents/caregivers.

While the scientific process offers a methodical approach to describing what exists, the design process offers a methodical approach to creating what doesn't exist. The design process adds structure to the problem-solving process to make project solutions more attainable. It also draws on many executive function skills, from following multiple steps to catching and correcting errors to anticipating outcomes to evaluating solutions, and more. Thus, using a design process contributes to the **climate of executive function**.

STOP! Turn to Your *Efficacy Notebook*

As you think of creating that home–school connection in your **Hybrid Learning Environment**, answer these questions.

1   How can you use home-based projects to enhance your curriculum?
2   What kinds of projects might students tackle at home that would be of interest to them and not require a lot of your involvement?
3   How might you involve your students in selecting a pursuit-based problem (Chapter 4) to tackle with some level of involvement from their parents/caregivers?

Resources

In school, students are surrounded by resources; it's important to provide similar access to resources at home. Help parents/caregivers help their children gather up the resources they will need in their learning, by providing a box, basket, or drawer in a Remote Learning Zone desk. Suggest they fill it with items such as pencils, pens, markers or crayons, highlighters, a ruler, compass, protractor, notepad, index cards, scissors, glue, etc. Obviously, the age of your students will determine the types of resources they need.

Some resources, such as those listed here, are physical. Consider the digital resources students can use, including the various reference subscriptions your school might have, such as dictionaries, atlases, encyclopedias, picture banks, thesauruses, etc. Design digital *How-To Sheets* and videos to guide students through skills they will need in the classroom. Kindergarten teachers: record videos for how to use scissors, how to use a glue stick, how to write each of the letters of the alphabet, and so forth. For older students, a *How-To Sheet* or *Video* can be created for setting up lab reports, applying paint in a watercolor painting, measuring an angle with a protractor, and so forth. See Figure 9.5 for an example. Create a digital *Resource Area* on your Learning Management System so all resources are easily accessed.

The key is to ensure that while students' brains are in the midst of grappling with content, they are not distracted by needing to leave their Remote Learning Zone to find resources. Everything should be at their fingertips.

How-to Add Fractions with Unlike Denominators

$$\frac{4}{7} + \frac{1}{5}$$

1   List out all of the multiples for each *denominator* … keep going until you find a number they have in common

    $7 \rightarrow$ 14, 21, 28, 35, 42, 49, …..
    $5 \rightarrow$ 10, 15, 20, 25, 30, 35, …..

2   Circle/highlight the multiple that they have in common.

    $7 \rightarrow$ 14, 21, 28, **35**, 42, 49, …..
    $5 \rightarrow$ 10, 15, 20, 25, 30, **35**, …..

3   Rewrite each of the fractions above so that they have the same denominator.

$$\frac{4}{7} = \frac{?}{35}$$

To get to 35 from 7, you have to multiply by 5. Since you multiplied the denominator by 5, you have to multiply the numerator by 5. You arrive at 20/35

$$\frac{4}{7} = \frac{20}{35}$$

$$\frac{1}{5} = \frac{7}{35}$$

Do the same for the fraction of ⅕. You have to multiply 5 by 7 to get to 35 so you have to do the same for the numerator.

4

$$\frac{20}{35} + \frac{7}{35} = \frac{27}{35}$$

Now that the fractions have the same denominator, you can add the numerators to obtain the answer. Next, you must ensure that the answer is in simplest form (there's a How-To Sheet for that if you don't know how to accomplish that).

Figure 9.5 Section of a *How-To Sheet*

Resources are an important complement to instruction, so help parents/caregivers help their children.

Sharing Limited Resources at Home

When students are working from home, they may have to compete with others for time with limited resources. Students may have to share a computing device, a favorite chair or desk, an electronic game device, a musical instrument, and more. To eliminate fighting, bullying, crying, and, well, you get the picture, use a *Limited Resource Sign-Up Sheet* (see Figure 9.6). Each family member (I like to start with the youngest) signs up to use the resource at a particular time. Each morning, family members can sign up for when they will use various resources. The student has to keep track of time and be ready to use the resource at the designated time and finish using it in time for the next person to start. Identifying the resources they need, deciding when would be the best time to use it, prioritizing resources in the selection process, and keeping track of time for when the resource is reserved all require and build executive function skills. This sign-up sheet also supports the SEL competencies of relationship skills and responsible decision-making.

Downtime

It's important for all of us to take a break from work at times to recharge through some exercise, deep breathing, meditation, music, and other activities. When students are working from home, in particular, it's easy to just sit in front of the computer all day and not get up! Encourage students and their parents/caregivers to build in some 10-minute breaks across the day. During those breaks, students should definitely get out of their seats to get some blood and oxygen flowing to the brain.

Teach your students a deep-breathing routine. Develop some easy, indoor exercise routines for them to follow. Invite them to find a way to recharge, perhaps by moving to some music, engaging in an art activity, engaging in mindfulness meditation, and more. After about 10 minutes, students can return to their work with their brains ready to tackle the next activity.

Two downtime activities are great for building creativity:

◆ Daydream: Just spend 5 to 10 minutes with your eyes closed and let your mind wander into any world you dream up.
◆ Observe: Stay inside or head outside and look at something for 5 to 10 minutes, just observing it. It could be the scene outside the window,

Limited Resource Sign-Up Sheet

Resource: _____

Please use the resource during the time allotted and BE SURE to complete your use on time. If you need more time you can sign up again at a later time.

Start Time	End Time	Your Name

Figure 9.6 *Limited Resource Sign-Up Sheet* for Sharing Resources at Home

which might include many activities. Or it could involve finding an item and looking at it very closely to notice everything about it.

Both daydreaming and observation build the executive function skill of creativity.

If you have your students schedule their day, have them schedule in several downtime breaks. Ensure that parents/caregivers know this is the plan.

Invite them to join their children in a deep-breathing or exercise break. Have students track how they use their downtime and graph it across a week, a month, and a year.

Conversation

A good conversation builds SEL, executive function, language skills, thinking skills, and more. It provides inspiration, questions, challenges, ideas, and answers. When students are learning from home, they may feel their parents/caregivers are always around; however, that doesn't mean they're engaging in conversation.

Let students and parents/caregivers know the importance of conversation. Provide them with some guidelines, such as taking a break and sitting down with one another, respecting all ideas and contributions to the conversation, refraining from criticizing one another, letting the student articulate thoughts and ideas on their own, ensuring that all involved in the conversation have the opportunity to speak, etc.

Give parents/caregivers some conversation starters. If students are younger, ask them about their studies (what they find easy and what they find more difficult), or have them share about something of which they are most proud. With older students, engage them in conversation to gain their ideas and insights on real-world issues. Ask them what the perfect school would be like, or if they were to write a book, what might they write about and why. Have them share their favorite songs and musical artists and explain why they favor them. Position parents/caregivers to incorporate regular, meaningful conversations into the home-based learning environment. Make conversations, both in and outside of school, a part of the **culture of social and emotional learning**.

Balance

Both structure and downtime might help here. We all need some balance in our day, and students may need guidance in that area. While you can offer that guidance, it's important to share your ideas with parents/caregivers as well so they can reinforce them.

School involves a variety of different types of activities throughout the day, including reading, writing, problem solving, computing, analyzing, speaking, listening, experimenting, moving, playing, engaging in sports, engaging in the arts, and more. Think about the home-based learning environment and students' existing mental models.

Students are used to completing homework at home. That usually consists of academic work. Some students like to come home from school and complete their homework immediately; others like to take a break, perhaps have dinner, and then sit down to work on it. Homework usually involves a chunk of time dedicated to the work.

When students are learning from home all day, it's important that they don't view the day as they do homework and squeeze it all into one time period. Throughout the day, students need some balance between more rigorous academic studies that require a lot of brain power; breaks; practice work; engagement in the arts, sports, or other movement activities; eating; and hydrating. It is important for students to avoid scheduling all their school activities together in the morning, for example, so they can have the afternoon to themselves, assuming they're not engaging with you or other teachers all day.

Have students track how they use their time each day, and, as with downtime, map the percentage of time they spend on each different kind of activity in a day. Let students demonstrate their mastery of the art of balance in their lives by graphing out a typical day and writing about how it felt to create balance among the various activities in which they engaged. This will not only enhance their school experience, but it will also create a mindset to last their whole lives.

Celebration Zone

Let's face it: we are all proud of our accomplishments. They make us feel capable and special. Teachers regularly celebrate their students' accomplishments with badges, awards, posting of their work, giving shout-outs to the success stories, and more. So, keep that spirit going in the home-based learning environment.

Encourage parents/caregivers to create a physical or virtual Celebration Zone. That might mean a bulletin board or designated spot on a wall. It might mean a digital portfolio. Encourage students to identify the schoolwork of which they are most proud in a day or week and post that to their Celebration Zone. Parents/caregivers can use the Celebration Zone as a conversation starter, asking students to share why they posted certain items.

It's important not to leave the celebration to the adult. Have the students identify and share items, thus building self-awareness in terms of their strengths, growth, and interests. Students should manage the Celebration Zone; parents/caregivers should ensure that one exists and engage with their children around it.

Reflection

As you learn, if you stop and think about what you learned, how it will help you, how you learn best, and so forth, you will help solidify that learning. Position parents/caregivers to build reflection into their home-based learning environment, potentially using it as a conversation starter.

Offer students and their parents/caregivers ideas for reflective practice, such as these:

- Using the *Great Hybrid Learner Rubric* to reflect daily on their growth as a strong student
- Reflecting at the end of each activity (as in the case of an *Efficacy Notebook*) on one to three points: what I learned; how I will use the learning; what new questions arose from this activity that I want to pursue; what I enjoyed about the activity; what could have made the activity even better; etc.
- Keeping a gratitude journal where the student can write about what they're grateful for each day
- Setting a daily goal for work habits and writing a sentence or two at the end of each day to reflect on progress

Reflection, and even journaling, help the brain build more connections among content. It is an important part of the home-based learning environment that parents/caregivers can encourage. Learning is not a matter of simply completing assignments; it's about incorporating the learning into our lives and discovering how to become an even better learner!

While you don't necessarily want parents/caregivers to provide instruction to their children, you can position them to play an important role as part of your **network of purposeful and productive facilitation of learning**. These eight elements of a home-based learning environment will create a sense of structure and purpose for students to excel in their learning.

 STOP! Turn to Your *Efficacy Notebook*

As you reflect on the eight elements of a home-based learning environment, answer these questions in your *Efficacy Notebook*.

1   What ideas do you have for establishing an effective home-based learning environment for your students?

2   How will you position parents/caregivers to manage this home-based learning environment?
3   How will you involve students in sharing with their parents/caregivers the goals and components of a home-based learning environment?

Reference

Vallat, R., Meunier, D., Nicolas, A., & Ruby, P. (2018). Hard to wake up? The cerebral correlates of sleep inertia assessed using combined behavioral, EEG and fMRI measures. *Neuroimage, 184*, 266–278.

Appendix

Great Hybrid Learner Rubric—Kindergarten

	Practicing	Got It!
I am ready to learn.	• I have the things I need to learn. pencil　　book device　　paper • I have a place to learn. desk　　table	All of *Practicing* plus: I help my friends get ready to learn!
I focus.	I stay on task. ☐ I look with my eyes. ☐ I listen with my ears. ☐ I keep my body still.	All of *Practicing* plus: I ask for help when I can't focus.
I work well with others.	☐ I share things and ideas. ☐ I use kind words.	All of *Practicing* plus: I help my friends when they need it.
I manage my time.	☐ I order my activities. ☐ I plan breaks.	All of *Practicing* plus: I explain how I plan my day to help my friends.
I am responsible with my work.	☐ I finish my work. ☐ I keep my work neat.	All of *Practicing* plus: When I finish early, I improve my work before turning it in.

Great Hybrid Learner Rubric—Grades 1–2

	Learning 😐	Practicing 🙂	Got It! 😄

I am ready to learn.	☐ I use the checklist to remind me to have my materials.
	☐ I need help finding a calming spot to get ready to learn.
		☐ I am ready for class with the tools I need to learn:
		  ☐ A device
		  ☐ My work
		  ☐ Books
		  ☐ Pencils
		  ☐ Other tools
		☐ I take a deep breath and sit in a calming spot to get ready to learn.
			All of *Practicing* plus:
			I check the class page for information from my teacher before getting to work.

I am responsible for my work.	☐ I need reminders to finish my work on time. ☐ I keep my papers in one space.	☐ I complete all of my work on time. ☐ I organize my work on paper and online so my teacher and I can find what I need.	All of *Practicing* plus: When I finish early, I improve my work before I turn it in.
I can focus.	☐ I need reminders to help me stay focused. ☐ I use one strategy or tool to help me stay on task.	☐ I stay on task. ☐ If I get distracted, I get back on task quickly. ☐ I keep off-task conversations for lunch or free time.	All of *Practicing* plus: I take responsibility to stay focused. I may move to a better space to help me focus.
I work well with others.	☐ I share my ideas. ☐ I need reminders to listen to others when they share their ideas.	☐ I work with my classmates to create class jobs. ☐ I share my ideas and look at group members' faces when we are talking. ☐ I listen to others when they share their ideas.	All of *Practicing* plus: I make sure that all group members have a chance to share their ideas. I ask questions to help me understand others.
I manage my time.	☐ I need help to plan my schedule. ☐ I try to stick with my schedule. ☐ I explain why some activities took a longer or shorter time.	☐ I plan my schedule all by myself. ☐ I complete activities within the time limits. ☐ I adjust my plan as needed while still meeting expectations. ☐ I plan breaks, and I plan time for my own creativity.	All of *Practicing* plus: I explain how I plan my time to help others.

Great Hybrid Learner Rubric—Grades 3–5: The Basics

	Novice	Apprentice	Practitioner	Expert
Managing Technology Access	❑ makes a list of logins and passwords so they can be easily found	❑ makes a list of logins and passwords for easy access ❑ tries to resolve technology issues first before asking for help	❑ makes a list of logins and passwords for easy access ❑ is resourceful in finding answers to technology issues (e.g., online searches, *how-to videos*, expert advice, etc.) ❑ persists in resolving technology issues	all of *Practitioner* plus creates a sign-up sheet for using any technology that is being shared in the house
Establishing Structures	❑ sets a plan for the day ❑ chooses a location in which to do schoolwork	❑ creates a schedule for each day ❑ schedules at least one movement or brain break ❑ creates a physical learning space	❑ creates a schedule for each day, including start/end times ❑ schedules time for movement, lunch, mindfulness, and other brain breaks ❑ creates a quiet and organized space that supports concentration	all of *Practitioner* plus establishes a digital and physical resource area

(Continued)

Great Hybrid Learner Rubric—Grades 3–5: The Basics (Continued)

	Novice	Apprentice	Practitioner	Expert
Reflection and Self-Assessment	❑ sets work habit goals each day ❑ self-assesses the ability to balance learning each day	❑ sets learning goals and work habit goals each day ❑ self-assesses at the end of each activity ❑ self-assesses time management each day	❑ sets learning goals and work habit goals each week ❑ self-assesses daily progress in meeting goals ❑ self-assesses daily success in using a schedule	all of *Practitioner* plus uses a *learning dashboard* to monitor progress
Engagement	❑ attends meetings with reminders ❑ makes activity choices	❑ attends meetings ❑ chooses activities with help from an adult ❑ makes choices about where and when *learning activities* are completed with help from an adult	❑ attends meetings on time ❑ makes thoughtful choices of activities and the order in which they are completed ❑ makes thoughtful choices about where and when *learning activities* are completed ❑ self-advocates by communicating needs and progress with the teacher	all of *Practitioner* plus suggests to the teacher possible *small-group mini-lessons* or areas where more support would help

Great Hybrid Learner Rubric—Grades 3–5: Your Role in the Classroom

	Novice	Apprentice	Practitioner	Expert
Collaboration and Social Awareness	☐ connects with the teacher for collaboration ☐ listens to others during whole group time	☐ connects with other students to collaborate via the teacher ☐ listens to others ☐ finds solutions to conflicts with others, with teacher support ☐ shows appreciation	☐ connects with other students to collaborate as assigned by the teacher ☐ actively listens to others ☐ finds solutions to conflicts with others ☐ shows appreciation ☐ makes suggestions to group members to work more effectively	all of *Practitioner* plus assists group members in reaching consensus and resolving conflict
Self-Regulation and Focus	☐ with prompting from teacher or peer, starts tasks ☐ with prompting from teacher or peer, resumes task and refocuses	☐ recognizes loss of focus and gets back on task without teacher, caregiver, or peer prompting ☐ when working independently, chooses a seat to minimize distractions	☐ stays on task throughout an activity or learning experience ☐ switches from one activity to the next with minimal "down time" ☐ resumes focus when distractions occur ☐ avoids distracting others ☐ reserves off-task conversations and messaging for non-discussion times	all of *Practitioner* plus develops strategies for effectively staying focused during school and homework

(Continued)

Great Hybrid Learner Rubric—Grades 3–5: Your Role in the Classroom (Continued)

	Novice	Apprentice	Practitioner	Expert
Working Through Challenges	❏ asks someone for help when questions or problems arise ❏ re-reads directions when prompted	❏ seeks out resources and appropriate people when questions or problems arise ❏ re-reads directions when stuck	❏ re-reads directions to double-check understanding ❏ virtually reaches out to peers for help if possible ❏ if unable to continue without help, moves on to something else productive	all of *Practitioner* plus connects with other students to offer help
Self-Care	❏ takes breaks throughout the day ❏ learns from mistakes	❏ takes breaks or seeks support in response to struggles ❏ maintains a growth mindset and learns from mistakes	❏ pauses to reflect on feelings throughout the day; takes breaks or seeks support in response ❏ maintains a growth mindset and learns from mistakes	all of *Practitioner* plus shares encouraging words with other people at home to help them stay positive

Great Hybrid Learner Rubric—Grades 6–8

	Novice	Apprentice	Practitioner	Expert
Management and Organization	☐ accesses login information with the teacher's support ☐ creates a schedule for each week ☐ creates a quiet space to work	☐ creates a list of login information (usernames and passwords) for necessary applications and learning platforms ☐ creates a schedule for each week ☐ creates a quiet space that supports concentration ☐ uses a rubric to determine learning goals	☐ creates a list of login information (usernames and passwords) for necessary applications and learning platforms; stores it in an easily accessible place ☐ creates a schedule for each week, including start/end times ☐ creates a quiet and organized space that supports concentration ☐ uses a rubric to determine learning goals and selects activities to support goals	all of *Practitioner* plus creates a digital resource page for a parent/caregiver of all the technology platforms
Self-Regulation	☐ stays on task through most of an activity or learning experience ☐ attends each learning experience ☐ asks questions	☐ stays on task throughout an activity or learning experience ☐ transitions between activities seamlessly with a prompt from the teacher ☐ attends each learning experience on time ☐ asks questions to aid in learning	☐ stays focused and on task throughout an activity or learning experience ☐ transitions between activities seamlessly without a prompt from the teacher ☐ attends each learning experience on time with all needed materials ☐ asks questions to aid in learning and communicates needs with the teacher	all of *Practitioner* plus uses focus cards to reflect on times when not on task and makes a plan to adjust

(Continued)

Great Hybrid Learner Rubric—Grades 6–8 (Continued)

	Novice	Apprentice	Practitioner	Expert
Social Awareness	☐ actively listens to others ☐ effectively works within the group	☐ actively listens to others ☐ shows appreciation for others ☐ makes suggestions about working effectively as a group ☐ avoids distracting others much of the time during learning experiences	☐ actively listens to others and follows up with comments that connect peers' points ☐ shows appreciation for others' support ☐ makes and listens to suggestions about working effectively as a group ☐ avoids distracting others during learning experiences	all of *Practitioner* plus reflects on how distractions impact the group or learning environment and shares strategies of how to limit them
Perseverance	☐ hands in quality work on time ☐ re-reads directions prior to reaching out for teacher support	☐ hands in quality work on time based on rubric expectations ☐ re-reads directions and accesses resources prior to reaching out for teacher support ☐ continues to try through setbacks	☐ consistently hands in quality work on time based on rubric expectations ☐ re-reads directions, reviews notes, and accesses resources prior to reaching out for teacher support ☐ continues to try through and after setbacks	all of *Practitioner* plus shares strategies with peer group to develop and maintain perseverance
Reflection	☐ maintains a growth mindset by reflecting on mistakes in learning ☐ reflects on learning goals each week with teacher support	☐ maintains a growth mindset by reflecting on mistakes in learning and behavior ☐ begins the day with a daily positive affirmation ☐ reflects on learning goals each week	☐ maintains a growth mindset by reflecting on and learning from mistakes in learning and behavior ☐ begins and ends the day with daily positive affirmations ☐ reflects on learning and work habit goals each week	all of *Practitioner* plus keeps a gratitude journal to reflect in each day

Great Hybrid Learner Rubric—Grades 9–12

	Novice	Apprentice	Practitioner	Expert
Resourcefulness	☐ works to stay focused during school ☐ reaches out for support to find answers to technology issues ☐ creates a weekly schedule including start/end times ☐ creates a quiet space to focus on academic work while at home	☐ develops strategies for staying focused during school ☐ utilizes a collection of resources to support finding answers to technology issues ☐ uses a rubric to determine learning goals ☐ creates a weekly schedule including start/end times, extracurricular activities, and job responsibilities to balance responsibilities of school and home ☐ creates a quiet space to focus and concentrate on academic work while at home	☐ develops strategies for effectively staying focused during school ☐ utilizes a collection of resources to support finding answers to and resolving technology issues ☐ uses a rubric to determine learning goals and thoughtfully selects activities to achieve those goals ☐ creates and manages a weekly schedule including start/end times, extracurricular activities, and job responsibilities to balance responsibilities of school and home ☐ creates a quiet, organized space to focus and concentrate on academic work while at home	all of *Practitioner* plus creates a digital resource area for sharing strategies
Resilience	☐ consistently self-checks assignments prior to submitting on time ☐ develops strategies to persist through challenges at school to achieve quality work products ☐ attends scheduled meetings	☐ consistently self-checks assignments prior to submitting on time ☐ develops strategies to persist through challenges at school to achieve quality work products ☐ promptly attends all scheduled meetings	☐ consistently and accurately self-checks assignments prior to submitting on time ☐ develops strategies to persist through challenges at school and home to achieve quality work products ☐ promptly attends all scheduled meetings with all needed materials	all of *Practitioner* plus establishes and utilizes a peer accountability partner

(Continued)

Great Hybrid Learner Rubric—Grades 9–12 (Continued)

	Novice	Apprentice	Practitioner	Expert
Social Awareness	☐ connects with other students in school ☐ actively listens to peers ☐ stays focused during class ☐ reserves off-task conversations and messaging for non-discussion times ☐ shows respect for teachers and peers	☐ connects with other students in school to collaborate on assignments ☐ actively and respectfully listens to peers ☐ resolves group conflicts respectfully ☐ shares strategies for effective group work ☐ stays focused during class so as not to distract from others' learning ☐ reserves off-task conversations and messaging for class transitions so as not to disrupt the learning environment ☐ leads *small-group mini-lessons* to support peers' learning ☐ shows respect for each member of the school community	☐ connects with other students in and out of school to collaborate on assignments ☐ actively and respectfully listens and responds to peers ☐ resolves group conflicts respectfully through consensus-building ☐ develops and shares strategies and norms for effective group work ☐ stays focused and on task during class so as not to distract from others' learning ☐ reserves off-task conversations and messaging for class transitions so as not to disrupt the learning environment ☐ leads *small-group mini-lessons* and designs resources to support peers' learning ☐ consistently shows respect for each member of the school community	all of *Practitioner* plus actively ensures various voices and perspectives are heard during class and extracurricular activities

Great Hybrid Learner Rubric—Grades 9–12 (Continued)

	Novice	Apprentice	Practitioner	Expert
Self-Care	❑ self-advocates by communicating needs and questions ❑ pauses to reflect on feelings throughout the day	❑ self-advocates by communicating needs and questions to appropriate adults within the school community ❑ pauses to reflect on feelings throughout the day, recognizing when feelings of stress or frustration are evident ❑ takes a moment during the day to be creative	❑ self-advocates by communicating needs, strengths, concerns, and questions to appropriate adults within the school community ❑ pauses to reflect on feelings throughout the day, recognizing when feelings of stress or frustration are evident; takes a break or seeks needed support ❑ takes moments throughout the day to be creative	all of *Practitioner* plus shares additional tips and strategies of how to maintain self-care
Reflection	❑ reflects on setbacks and develops strategies to overcome obstacles ❑ begins day with positive affirmations ❑ creates academic or behavioral goals before each marking period ❑ maintains a growth mindset	❑ reflects on setbacks and develops strategies to overcome obstacles; seeks support from trusted adults within the school community ❑ begins day with positive affirmations ❑ creates academic and/or behavioral goals before each marking period; reflects on progress at the end of each marking period ❑ maintains a growth mindset and learns from mistakes	❑ reflects on and analyzes failures and setbacks; develops strategies to overcome obstacles; seeks support from trusted adults within the school community ❑ begins and ends day with positive affirmations ❑ creates academic and behavioral goals before each marking period; reflects on progress at the end of each marking period; makes adjustments to goals throughout the year ❑ maintains a growth mindset; learns from and takes ownership of mistakes	all of *Practitioner* plus keeps a daily reflection and gratitude journal

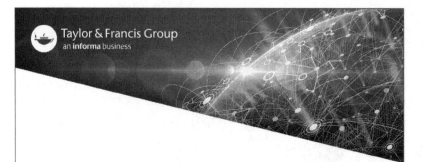